Understanding
GOLF

Philip Moore

This book is dedicated to my son Philip.

For always making me a proud father. And for taking the time from his busy schedule to design and build my wonderful golf shops.

Everything that can be counted does not necessarily count; everything that counts cannot necessarily be counted.

Albert Einstein

It's unbelievable how much you don't know about a game you've been playing all of your life.

Mickey Mantle

Understanding Golf

Opening thoughts

PART ONE: Understanding yourself as a golfer

PART TWO: Understanding golf as a game

PART THREE: Understanding golf clubs

PART FOUR: Understanding ball flight

PART FIVE: Understanding the golf swing

PART SIX: Understanding how to play better golf

Final thoughts

OPENING THOUGHTS

The average golfer's problem is not so much a lack of ability as it is a lack of knowing what he should do.

Ben Hogan

Why golfers stop improving.

Once in a while it really hits people that they don't have to experience the world in the way they have been told to.

Alan Keightley

I f you've been struggling for a long time to lower your average score, you're either playing to your maximum potential or you don't fully understand how golf is best played.

Golfers have been told that lower scores are achieved *primarily* through purchasing *better* equipment, developing a *better* golf swing and hitting the ball *farther*. Unfortunately, that most common approach takes you only so far.

With regards to the value of *better* equipment, today's average player uses far superior equipment and is scoring about the same as the average golfer did 30 years ago. That's because golf is not about technology. **Golf clubs don't select shots, read greens or swing themselves.**

With regards to the value of developing a *better* golf swing, can you even define what a *better* golf swing is? If you took lessons from three successful PGA teaching professionals, I can almost guarantee that you'd receive three different opinions on how to *better* your golf swing. None of the opinions would be wrong; it's just that every instructor has his or her own ideas about how you should swing a golf club. In truth, there are an unlimited number of ways for you to *effectively*

2

swing a golf club. If you watched the top 100 players in the world play golf, you'd see 100 noticeably different golf swings. The ball doesn't respond to how you swing, it only responds to the clubface at impact. ***Exactly how you swing doesn't matter.***

With regards to hitting the golf ball *farther*, golf is not a long drive contest. Improved golf is related primarily to improved accuracy and distance *control*, not increased distance. Golfers who strive to hit the ball farther, generally only succeed in hitting the ball farther off-line. ***Without improved accuracy and distance control, hitting the ball a little farther provides no advantage at all.***

When you focus exclusively on swing technique, equipment and distance, **you'll eventually just stop improving.**

A round of golf consists of a series of different shots played from different situations. It's not about the mindless repetition of a single motion with an expensive golf club. It's about *creating* the specific shot needed at a particular time. *Playing golf* is about shot selection and execution. You become a better *player* through becoming a better manager and shotmaker; specifically through becoming more proficient at each of the five *playing skills*: shot selection, club selection, intention, setup position and swing focus.

When a golfer stops developing his playing skills, **he permanently limits his potential as a golfer.**

Why Improvement is so easy

Thinking must be the hardest thing we do in golf, because we do so little of it.

Harvey Penick

W hy the average golfer struggles to improve becomes obvious when you analyze his approach to shotmaking.

Shot Selection

Skilled players aim away from difficult or penalizing situations, and primarily to the middle or safe side of fairways and greens.

Believing that they hit the ball far straighter than they actually do, average golfers too often aim directly at the hole. They routinely find themselves in penalizing or difficult situations because they make little effort to avoid those situations.

Club Selection

Skilled players always select a club that provides a margin of error. Allowing for the slight mishit (everyone's normal shot), they never *under- club* themselves.

Believing they hit the ball longer than they actually do, average golfers continually *under-club* themselves. This leads to over swinging, poor distance control, and a high percentage of mishits.

Intention

After selecting their shot and before addressing the ball, skilled players establish a clear positive intention to create that exact shot.

Average golfers typically think about the shots they *don't* want to create or things they *don't* want to do. They might think, "Don't slice it", "Don't hit it in the lake", "Don't move your head" or "Don't swing too hard". Those thoughts create correspond- ing mental images that actually make the undesirable outcome more likely.

Set up Position

Skilled golfers understand how the various aspects of their set up position

(ball position, grip alignment, shoulder alignment, and stance) directly influence impact conditions. As a result, they make a conscious effort to always set up to the ball in the manner that would allow them to most easily create their intended shot.

Average golfers have no idea how their set up position influ- ences their ball-striking. They seldom make square and cen- tered contact because they seldom get themselves properly set up to the ball.

Swing Focus

While maintaining the intention to create a specific shot, skilled players allow their swing to unfold as naturally as possible. They swing with intention, trust, and confidence; not thought.

Average golfers cannot stop thinking while they are swinging. Fearing a mishit, they always try to consciously manipulate their golf swing. As a result, their swing motion is unnatural, off-bal- anced and highly inconsistent.

Considering the quality of his playing skills, it amazes me that the average golfer plays as well as he does.

It also becomes abundantly clear **how easy it would be for him to improve.**

About this book

I believe all golfers have the ability to immediately lower their average score, without changing their swing or equipment. All they need to do is further develop their playing skills.

Fortunately, each of the five playing skills is within the golfer's complete conscious control. Therefore, improvement does not require greater than average physical talent or months on the practice tee. What IS required is an understanding of golf that most golfers don't possess.

As a result of being preoccupied with their swing mechanics, the quality of their equipment, and how far they hit the ball, modern golfers tend to have a surprisingly limited understanding of how the game is best played. The purpose of this book is to address that specific issue.

I wrote this book with three objectives in mind. First, I wanted the book to be short and easy to read. Second, I wanted to significantly expand the readers understanding of golf as a game. Third, I wanted to provide the reader with the tools needed to immediately lower his or her average score.

That's it. That's what this book is all about. I hope you enjoy it and I'll look forward to hearing from you.

Phil
PhilMooreGolf.com

PART ONE
UNDERSTANDING
YOURSELF AS A GOLFER

Often, when we are trying to take strokes off our score, we attach too much importance to new theories of the swing, and overlook the fact that we are not getting everything we should out of the mechanical ability already possessed.

Bobby Jones

If you keep recycling the same thoughts, **you'll keep producing the same scores.**

We can't solve problems by using the same kind of thinking we used when we created them.

Albert Einstein

We create success or failure on the course primarily by our thoughts.

Gary Player

We have about 60,000 thoughts a day and about 95% of those thoughts never change, which is why our lives evolve into such a rut. I don't know how many thoughts you have during a round of golf, but I guarantee they don't change much, *which is why you struggle to improve.*

Regardless of your level of play, if you want to score better you have to think better. There is no other way, the same thoughts will always produce the same scores.

Golf is a game. The object is to get the ball into the hole in as few shots as possible. As long as you abide by the rules, *how* you do it doesn't matter. The techniques you employ, the equipment you use, and how far you hit the ball, are all irrelevant. At the end of the round you add up the numbers on the score card and the player with the lowest total wins.

Before Tiger Woods came along, the overwhelming consensus was that Jack Nicklaus was the greatest player in the history of golf. Yet I never heard of one expert who felt that Nicklaus had the best swing, was the best ball striker, or that he played with the best equipment. He won 18 professional major championships, more than any other golfer in history, for one reason - *he knew how to get the ball into the hole in fewer strokes than anyone else.*

Jack Nicklaus was an exceptional putter and very long off the tee; but he said that of all his scoring weapons, **his strongest was his mind** - what and how he thought about the game.

In truth, every great champion attributes their success *not to technique or equipment*, but to their mental approach to the game.

Most golfers think as little as possible on the golf course. You might say they play on *automatic pilot.* Their entire approach to golf could be summed up as follows:

> **On Course Management:** *When they cannot reach the green, they aim in the general direction of the fairway, use a driver and swing hard. When they can reach the green, they aim directly at the flagstick, use the shortest club possible and swing hard.*

> **On Swing Management:** *When swinging, they think of the last swing-thought that seemed to work. After each mishit, they replace that swing-thought, with another thought that worked for awhile in the past.*

That's it. That's how they play golf. When you approach each shot in the same manner and allow each swing to be guided by the same recycled thoughts, you're going to keep producing the same scores.

In physics, the *principle of complementarity* says that when you look at something from a certain perspective, that's what you see; when you look at it from a different perspective, you see something different.

On the golf course, when considering a golf shot, **different players see different things.**

Consider two golfers with equal ball-striking ability and the same equipment playing the identical second shot to a par-4. The shot is 130-yards over water to a flagstick located very close to the front left corner of the green.

The first player believes that he hits his 8-iron exactly 130 yards, so he considers this a birdie opportunity and aims directly at the flag. Concerned about the water, he tells himself to keep his head down and swing hard.

What he fails to consider is that he only hits his 8-iron 130 yards when he makes perfect contact – *which neither he nor anyone else does very often.* Furthermore, his fear of the water and manipulative swing thoughts only serve to produce added stress and tension – *making the shot more difficult to execute.*

For the increased chance of making a 3, he has greatly increased the possibility of making a much higher score.

The second player sees the same shot differently. He fully understands that a well struck 8-iron aimed directly at the flag would provide an increased *chance* to make a birdie. But, he also understands that a mishit 8-iron could easily find the water and probably result in at least a double bogie. Furthermore, a *slightly pulled* 8-iron to the left of the green would leave him with a very difficult chip (because he'd have little green to work with) and a probable bogie. He reduces the possibility of being short or left by selecting a 7-iron and aiming to the right of the flag. Carrying the water no longer requires perfect contact, he's aiming further away from the left side of the green, and he'll still be left with a birdie putt.

His chance of executing the shot is also improved because he doesn't have to deal with the stress and tension associated with trying to hit a perfect golf shot – *he has provided himself with adequate room for error.*

While maintaining the possibility of making a 3, he has greatly reduced the possibility of making a much higher score.

So what you have here are two players with the same equipment and similar ball-striking ability, but very different handicaps.

Different because they **think differently**, they see shots differently.

Bobby Jones wrote, *"There is not a single hole that can't be birdied if you just think. But there is also not one that can't be doubled bogeyed if you ever stop thinking.*

If you don't change your beliefs, **you'll keep recycling the same thoughts.**

It ain't what you don't know that gets you in trouble. It's what you know for sure that just ain't so.

Mark Twain

Albert Einstein is credited with stating that the most important decision a person can make is whether the universe is friendly or hostile. He was referring to the incredible influence of *core belief;* specifically how that most fundamental *core belief* would directly influence how a person perceived and dealt with every aspect of his or her life.

Now consider your *beliefs* about golf, the process of improvement, and your ability as a golfer. ***Every thought, emotion, and action that you have on the golf course stems from those beliefs.***

With regards to lowering your average score, most golfers believe the following:

> ***Lowering your average score is difficult because golf is a very difficult game.***

> ***To lower your average score you have to develop a better golf swing.***

14

To lower your average score you have to hit more good shots per round.

You'll score lower if you hit the ball farther.

You'll score lower if you purchase the newest equipment.

Your scoring potential is limited by your physical talent.

These all sound true, but are they?

Lowering your average score is difficult because golf is a very difficult game.

Holding this belief serves no purpose other than to justify long term struggle with little or no improvement.

All golfers are, to some degree, limited in their understanding of how to lower their average score. It's that limited understanding, not the game itself, which inhibits their improvement.

In truth, lowering your average score is not difficult – once you acquire a better understanding of how to do it.

To lower your average score you have to develop a better golf swing.

Believing that a better golf swing automatically produces lower scores is based on the false belief that *playing golf* and the *golf swing* are one and the same.

Through improving your shot selection and developing a more efficient approach to shot making, you'll lower your average score significantly with the golf swing you currently have.

And if you don't improve in those areas, you can change your golf swing a hundred times and never lower your average score.

To lower your average score you have to hit more good shots per round.

That sounds logical, but it's not true. Furthermore, endlessly striving to hit perfect golf shots creates added tension, frustration and self-doubt.

In truth, poor shots hurt your score far more than good shots help your score. And hitting fewer poor shots per round doesn't require endless practice; it only requires improved shot selection and a more effective *approach* to shot-making.

Regardless of your level of play, when you start to replace poor shots with average shots your average score will drop.

You'll score lower if you hit the ball farther.

Golf is not a long drive contest. Simply hitting the ball farther will not automatically produce lower scores. The essence of good golf is distance *control*, not raw distance.

Without distance control, the long hitter has no advantage at all.

You'll score lower if you purchase the newest equipment.

If purchasing new equipment lowered your average score, you could improve every year by doing nothing more than purchasing the newest equipment.

Your ability to score is limited by your understanding of the game, not your equipment.

You can, however, learn to significantly lower your average score with the equipment you already have.

Your scoring potential is limited by your physical talent.

Holding this belief leads the player to feeling helpless and generates thoughts of giving-up. How can you improve if you believe you don't have the talent to improve?

Golfers with severe physical handicaps have won major championships simply because they fully understood their game and acquired a deep understanding of how golf is best played.

In truth, no golfer has ever played to their maximum physical ability. You haven't even approached your physical potential.

It is quite possible that your current beliefs about golf **are greatly inhibiting your ability to improve**.

Regardless of how you swing or how much you practice, **your swing will change slightly on a daily basis.**

It's a game of adjustments, a game of constant change and adjustment.
Ben Hogan

Whenever you come to the golf course, you bring a different body and a different mindset. Your weight, energy level, flexibility and frame of mind are always changing.

While these changes may be slight, they'll produce a **slightly changed golf swing.**

When warming up on the practice range, prior to a tournament round, Jack Nicklaus said his goal was to answer the simple question, *"What are my parameters today?"* His primary concern was to determine the quality of his game on that given day. Based on his ball striking ability *while warming up*, he would formulate his game plan for that day. If his ball striking was slightly off, he would alter his approach to both club and shot selection. He refers to his ability to score well without his best game as the learned ability to *"Play badly well"*.

The great Byron Nelson wrote, *"The first step in building a solid, dependable attitude is to be realistic, not only about your inherent capabilities, but also about how well you are playing to those capabilities on any given day."*

In his book, *How I Play Golf*, Tiger Woods writes, *"My swing tendencies change a bit from day to day. That's part of golf; for no discernible reason your misses might one day be pulls to the left, the next day fades a bit too far to the right. These small shifts in ball flight aren't necessarily disastrous, provided you allow for them"*. Tiger Woods routinely speaks of having his "A-game" one day and his "B-game" or "C-game" the next day. He accepts it and understands it to be, *"Just part of golf"*.

In his book, *Making the Turn*, PGA Senior Touring Professional Frank Beard writes about the importance of asking yourself, *"How do I feel today?" "Who am I today?" "What's going on today?"*

The average golfer and the touring professional have at least one thing in common - ***their golf swing changes slightly on a daily basis***.

The professional, by necessity, **embraces change** and learns how to effectively deal with it. The average golfer **resists change** and struggles endlessly as a result.

A slightly changed swing motion will most often produce a significant change in ball flight. There are two ways to effectively deal with that. You can either go with the ball flight you're creating and alter your shot selection for the day. Or you can slightly adjust your setup position in an effort *realign* your swing motion.

In his book, *Natural Golf*, Seve Ballesteros outlines each aspect of his setup position. He starts by writing, *"All of these factors, however, are subject to change, which is why it is crucial, when you warm up before a round, to try to identify changes in your swing, either by feel or by studying the ball's flight, or a combination of the two. Then, go ahead and move the ball around in your stance until you find the best position for playing the various clubs (on that given day)..."*

Notice that Seve did not recommend that you try to make changes to your golf swing on a daily basis. ***Instead, he recommended that (if needed) you slightly alter your setup position in an effort to bring it into balance with the swing motion you're creating on that given day.***

Your swing is guided by and moves around your setup position. ***It is possible, therefore, to "realign" your swing motion through slightly altering your setup position.***

Normally, only a *slight adjustment* in your grip, ball position, or shoulder alignment will be enough. To do this effectively, you need a basic understanding of how impact conditions create ball flight and how your setup position influences impact conditions (both will be addressed later in the book). The point I'm trying to stress here is that a changing swing motion is a fundamental aspect of golf. ***Expect your swing to change slightly on a daily basis and learn how to effectively deal with it.***

Consistency grows only after you **accept** and learn to **effectively manage** change.

Preparation is about 80% of the shotmaking process, **but golfers are seldom fully prepared before they swing.**

If you fail to prepare, you're preparing to fail.
John Wooden

In his book, *The Full Swing,* Jack Nicklaus writes, *"...how effectively you swing a golf club depends almost entirely on how well you have prepared to do so. All the finest players learned early in their careers that the quality of the swing is dependent about 80 percent on preparation and 20 percent on execution."*

A successful drive for Jack Nicklaus might have been 290 yards to a particular section of the fairway. A successful drive for you might be 200 yards anywhere in the fairway. ***The difference in talent level is irrelevant.***

The point is that the successful outcome of each of those shots was related **primarily** to how well you or he **prepared** to hit the shot.

Unfortunately, most golfers give little thought to preparation. Instead, they consider it more important to focus almost exclusively on the swing itself.

Nicklaus, however, felt the swing unfolded best when left alone. He writes, *"An effective golf swing is above all else a continuous flow of motion, and the less you need to dissect or direct it while actually playing the game, the better the motion will be — and the better swing you'll make."*

When Nicklaus speaks of preparation he is referring primarily to *intention* and *setup position*. Before hitting a golf shot, he would strengthen his intention through visualizing the exact shot he intended to hit. Then, he would meticulously assume the setup position that would allow him to most easily create that shot. Finally, while maintaining his intention to make contact with the golf ball in a particular manner, he would allow his swing to unfold as freely as possible.

Guided by and moving around his setup position, his swing was an **unrestricted seamless response** to his intention.

The importance of proper preparation pertains not only to full shots, but to every shot played. Just as Nicklaus would visualize the flight of a perfectly struck drive prior to addressing the ball, he would also visualize the ball dropping into the hole prior to addressing even the shortest putt.

And just as meticulous as he was in preparing to hit a long iron over water, *he was equally meticulous in preparing to hit the simplest chip.*

While golfers focus intently on their swing motion, the outcome of every golf shot is **determined primarily by the quality of their preparation.**

Creating a specific result starts with forming a specific intention, **which few golfers ever do.**

Winners see what they want. Losers see what they don't what.

Moe Norman

A man paints with his brain and not with his hand.

Michaelangelo

Your *intention* is the intangible aspect of shot-making. Because it can't be seen or felt, it is seldom even considered. That's a huge mistake because nothing will influence your swing motion more than your intention.

In his classic book, *Golf My Way*, Jack Nicklaus writes, *"I feel that hitting specific shots – playing the ball to a certain place in a certain way – is 50 percent mental picture…"* In other words, Nicklaus felt the 50% of the success of a golf shot was related to his ability to form a strong intention. *50 percent.*

Few golfers are aware of their intention **and even fewer understand the consequences of a poor intention.**

After hitting a particularly bad shot, ask yourself *exactly* what you had intended to do. Your intention was probably something along the lines of *"Hit it hard"*, *"Keep your head down"* or *"Don't slice it"*. Those well meant intentions will certainly influence your swing motion, but most often not in the way you had hoped.

The intention to *"Hit it hard"* usually results in a quick, off-balanced swing. As a result, a lot of shots *hit hard* fly into sand traps, lakes, trees and out-of-bounds.

The intention *"Keep your head down"* often creates a restricted back-swing and an overly steep downswing, resulting in a weak shot with the clubhead often striking the ground before the ball.

The intention *"Don't slice it"* often produces an even greater slice. In an effort to stop the ball from flying to the right, the golfer intuitively swings the clubhead further toward the left. The result being that the clubhead cuts across the target line to a greater degree than normal, producing greater slice spin than normal.

Shot-making becomes significantly easier when you employ the power of intention in a **beneficial manner;** and that requires nothing more than **common sense.**

A beneficial intention is positive…

We think in pictures and our body responds to those pictures. The thought, *"Don't hook the ball into the lake"* will create a mental vision of the ball hooking into the lake. The thought, *"Don't be short"* will create a mental vision of the putt stopping short of the hole. These are actually negative intentions. The problem is that your mind can't envision the word "don't".

24

Jack Nicklaus said that he never missed a putt in his mind. He was referring to the fact that he never addressed a putt before first visualizing it going into the hole. He always forms a *positive intention* prior to every shot.

To use the power of intention effectively, you need to forget about what you **don't want to happen** and focus exclusively on what you **do want to happen.**

A beneficial intention is single minded...

Some golfers try to balance a positive intention with a negative intention. While addressing their ball in the sand trap they might be thinking, *"I want to get the ball out of the trap, but I don't want to hit the ball over the green."* On the tee they might be thinking, *"I want to hit this drive as long as possible, but I don't want to slice it out-of-bounds."* In each instance, they formed two intentions, not one.

It's certainly good to consider all the possibilities, *but do that before you finalize your intention.* Your final intention should be positive and *single minded.* You should always form the single positive intention to hit your ball to a specific location on the green or fairway. **Given conflicting intentions, your brain sends conflicting signals through your motor nerves, creating a result that will seldom be what you were hoping for.**

A beneficial intention is highly specific...

George Knudsen, said that golf was a game of A to B. He meant that golf consisted of a series of shots *played one at a time* and always with the *intention* of hitting to a *specific point.* Hitting the ball from point-A to point-B.

The intention of hitting your drive into the fairway is not hitting your ball to a specific point. How do you align yourself and swing the clubhead directly at a 50 yard wide fairway? You can only align yourself and swing the clubhead at a specific point in the fairway.

The intention to hit a 3500 square foot green is also not hitting the ball to a specific point. You can only align yourself and swing the clubhead at a specific point on the green.

Your body responds to your intention. *If you're looking for a specific result, give your body a specific intention.*

A beneficial intention is external...

Most golfers *hope* to hit their targets by forming the intention to move their body in a particular manner. They might form the intention to keep their head still, or swing slowly, or turn the hips to start the forward swing. *These types of intentions are body oriented –* **internally focused.**

When you form the intention to consciously manipulate the movements of your body, you'll only succeed in creating an unnatural, inconsistent, off-balanced motion. Furthermore, the ball doesn't respond to how you move your body, it only responds to the clubface at impact.

The clubhead's target is the ball and the ball's target is the hole or specific location on the fairway or green. *Intend* to swing the golf club and strike the ball in the exact manner that will send the ball to your target. Then allow your body to naturally respond to that intention. *Your primary intention should always be target or impact oriented – externally focused.*

A beneficial intention is comfortable...

If you carry your 3-wood an average of 200 yards, you're probably not going to *feel comfortable* with the intention of hitting your 3-wood 215 yards over a lake.

If you slice every shot you hit, you're not going to *feel comfortable* with the intention of hitting a slight draw just because the flag happens to be on the left side of the green.

Discomfort creates tension, which inhibits your body's ability to efficiently respond to your intention. The shots you feel comfortable with will vary from day to day and sometimes within a single round. *Listen to your body and select the shot you can execute with the most comfort and confidence.*

A beneficial intention is strong...

Your intention has to be maintained throughout the shot-making process. It should be allowed to guide both how you setup to the ball and how you swing the clubhead. *To be effective, your intention has to be strong.*

Understanding this, better players use some technique to *strengthen* their intention before every shot. They might verbalize it, visualize it, or sense making perfect impact with soft practice swings.

Discover the technique that works best for you and make that technique an integral part of your approach to shot-making. *First you form a specific intention and then you strengthen that intention.*

That seems like a lot to think about, but it's actually less to think about. You focus *only* on creating the impact conditions that will send the ball to a specific target, strengthen that intention, and forget about everything else. What could be simpler?

Intention is the intangible aspect of shotmaking that is critically important, poorly understood **and seldom considered**

Of all the obstacles a golfer faces, **fear can be the most difficult to overcome.**

Fear of any kind is the number one enemy of all golfers, regardless of ball-striking and shot-making capabilities.
Jack Nicklaus

The highest quality that a human being can reach is to be independent from the good opinion of others.
Abraham Maslow

With fear, golf is no longer a manageable game. The golfer becomes preoccupied with where *not to go* and what *not to do*. The result being, as famed golf instructor Butch Harmon once said, *"…we get so afraid of hitting bad shots, we don't let ourselves hit good ones"*.

Fear does not make you a weak person – it's universal, everyone experiences it.

Our brain is hard wired to **instantaneously respond** to anything perceived to be threatening.

That's why the emotion of fear is often realized before one is able to rationally think about what is producing it.

The area of the brain known as the *amygdala* controls the autonomic responses associated with fear. **Once stimulated, it releases chemicals and stress hormones into the blood stream that trigger immediate emotional and physical responses.** Typically, your heart beats faster, your blood pressure increases, blood flows away from your extremities, your pupils dilate, and your mind races. You may also sense your fingers trembling, your stomach fluttering, and your mouth starting to dry.

Furthermore, when the amygdala is stimulated, access to the cortex (the thinking part of the brain) becomes restricted and sometimes even shuts down! Suddenly our perceptions change and decisions become more difficult to make. For the golfer, the fairway might *appear* narrower, the hole smaller, and breaks on the green more severe.

This subconscious response to perceived threatening circumstances stems from a primal self-preservation instinct. It's part of our DNA and it's commonly referred

to as the *fight or flight response*. While it may have served our distant ancestors well, it can be very difficult to deal with on the golf course.

A golfer in a state of fear will suddenly find himself **playing with a different mind and a different body**.

Eckhart Tolle writes in his book, *Practicing the Power of Now*, "...psychological fear is always of something that might happen, not of something that is happening now. You are in the here and now, while your mind is in the future... You can always cope with the present moment, but you cannot cope with something that is only a mind projection — you cannot cope with the future."

Fear arises on the golf course when the player becomes **emotionally attached to the outcome of a shot**. When they become overly concerned with what **might happen in the future**.

PGA touring professional, Brad Faxon, writes, *"Kids have no fear when they putt. They miss it and it doesn't affect them. You've got to keep that attitude your whole life. That's my whole premise toward putting. If you care whether you miss, you're in trouble."*

Teaching guru Dave Pelz writes, *"Golfers who don't care if they miss never get the yips."*

Most golfers don't think much about fear because they don't consider it to be a major concern. They feel it from time to time throughout their round, but they simply play through it. The problem is that even a mild fear can directly affect a player's perception and motor skills. ***If not confronted, fear will, to some degree, permanently inhibit their ability to improve.***

Fear does not go away through ignoring it. It goes away when you remove the stimulus. ***Fear is a natural subconscious response to something you have chosen to identify as threatening.*** Fortunately, you have the ability to change your perspective. Therefore, you have the ability to no longer perceive a particular circumstance as being threatening.

You can **remove the stimulus**.

This is what Gardner Dickinson was referring to when he wrote, *"To win, you must treat a pressure situation as an opportunity to succeed, not an opportunity to fail."*

The great Harry Vardon wrote, *"I have never been troubled by nerves in golf because I felt I had nothing to lose and everything to gain."*

Golfers tend to play to the level of their expectations, **and most golfers have very low expectations.**

A person who doubts himself is like a man who would enlist the ranks of his enemies and bear arms against himself. He makes his failure certain by himself being the first person convinced of it.

Alexander Dumas

If I have lost confidence in myself I have the universe against me.

Ralph Waldo Emerson

Self-doubt is not fear. You can have absolutely no fear of a golf shot and still doubt your ability to execute it. The average golfer can make 20 short putts in a row, miss one and then doubt his ability to make the next.

Based on past experiences, your brain determines your ability to make a particular golf shot. All past experiences, however, are not given the same consideration.

Golfers tend to remember mishits, **especially severe mishits**, more vividly than good shots.

Most golfers feel that if you practice and play, you should be able to learn how to hit good golf shots. As a result, a good golf shot is often not given much consideration. A short putt, for example, is normally tapped-in and retrieved from the cup without thought. *As if the shot had never happened.*

A missed short putt, however, is not expected. You weren't trying to miss it, so what happened? Did you miss-read it? Did you forget to align the putter face? Did the putter turn in your hand? Did it hit a bump on the green? *You leave the green feeling confused, frustrated and a little embarrassed.*

The 20 short putts that you made were given no thought; the one missed putt evoked strong negative emotions and detailed consideration. It's no wonder that the next short putt is approached with some degree of *self-doubt.* Jack Nicklaus wrote, *"It takes hundreds of good golf shots to gain confidence, but only one bad one to lose it."*

Fortunately, we can consciously choose **how we experience** our results.

You could have perceived the 21 short putts very differently. You could have chosen to feel good about each of the putts you made. And you could have attributed the missed putt to nothing more than a lack of focus and given it no further thought. *In other words, you could have treated the missed putt as if it had never happened.*

Very few golfers think this way, but some do.

In their outstanding book, *Every Shot Must Have A Purpose,* Pia Nilsson and Lynn Marriott discuss the importance of learning how to *associate* and *dissociate.* They write, *"To experience something emotionally is to be ASSOCIATED; to do so without emotional involvement means that you are DISSOCIATED. If you can teach yourself to associate with the good things and dissociate from the bad, your game will improve dramatically over time".*

Average golfers tend to approach every shot
with some degree of self doubt.

Doubting their ability to execute the shot, they try to recall what they did *wrong* the last time they faced a similar shot. Then they focus on making the corrections that'll hopefully produce a better result.

Champion golfers take the opposite approach. They try to instill *positive expectations* as part of their pre-shot routine.

PGA Tour professional Fred Couples says that when facing a particular golf shot, he remembers the *feel* of a similar shot that he executed successfully. When facing an 8-iron second shot to a par-4, he remembers the last time he hit a successful 8-iron. He takes a practice swing and vividly recalls the experience. Then he forms the intention of merely duplicating what he has already done.

LPGA superstar Annika Sorenstam says that she approaches every shot as though it was no different than similar shots that she has successfully executed thousands of times before. In 2003 she played against male golfers at the Bank of America Colonial tournament in Fort Worth, Texas. She was the first woman in nearly 60 years to play in a PGA Tour event. On the first tee, the world was watching and she felt enormous pressure. Before teeing-off, she just kept telling herself that it was just another 3-wood shot, just like the ones she'd hit successfully a thousand times before – *no different at all.* Then she *let go* and hit it perfectly.

Champion golfers make a conscious effort to create a *positive expectation*, and then let go. Average golfers create *self-doubt*, and can't let go.

Sports psychologists commonly use the term "Self-Efficacy", it roughly corresponds to a person's belief in their own competence. Sports psychologists universally accept that an athlete's *ability to succeed* is directly related to that athlete's *belief in their ability to succeed.* As Arnold Palmer once said, *"Your performance has a way of living up to your expectations".*

Moe Norman would repeatedly say, *"A bad shot wasn't in my mind. Every time I got over the ball I wondered how good it was going to be. I knew it was going to be good. But how good?"*

Swinging with confidence and positive expectations increases your chance of success. **So why would you ever swing without confidence and positive expectations?**

PART TWO
UNDERSTANDING GOLF AS A GAME

I have always thought that if a game was worth playing at all, it was worth making some effort to play it correctly.

Bobby Jones

Playing golf is not about perfect shot-making, **playing golf is about controlling mishits.**

Golf is a game of misses. The guy who misses the best is going to win.

Ben Hogan

Golf is not a game of great shots. It's a game of the most misses. The people who win make the smallest mistakes.

Gene Littler

In a 1993 Golf Magazine article, Jack Nicklaus wrote, *"The fact is, even at the highest levels of golf, perfect shots are mostly accidental and extremely rare. For instance, Ben Hogan, who was probably golf's all-time top perfectionist, reckoned he hit only a handful of shots per round exactly the way he wanted. Even at my best, I feel the same about my game."*

Bobby Jones wrote, *"I never did any real amount of winning until I learned to adjust my ambitions to more reasonable prospects. In a season's play I could perform at my best rate for not over a half-dozen rounds. In any one of these best rounds I would not strike more than six shots, other than putts, exactly as I intended."*

Tiger Woods wrote, *"I won 12 times in the year 2000, including 3 majors and I only remember hitting one shot I would call perfect. It was a 3 wood on number 14 in the third round of the British Open at St. Andrews."*

There are two reasons that perfect golf shots so rare, **even amongst the world's finest players.**

First, perfect shots require perfect contact.

Perfect contact requires that, *at the moment of impact*, the speed of the clubhead, the line on which the clubhead is traveling, the orientation of the clubface, and the exact point of impact on the clubface are all perfect. When that does happen, it is, as Jack Nicklaus writes, *mostly by accident.*

Second, you have no control over what might happen to the ball after it leaves the clubface.

Even if you do happen to make perfect contact, you can only guess at how the air and ground will affect the flight, bounce and roll of the ball.

Other than the occasional dropped putt, you need to accept that you'll hit very few, and normally no, perfect golf shots.

But that's okay, because you don't have to hit perfect golf shots **to play great golf.**

Golf courses do not demand perfection. Fairways are usually at least 40 to 50 yards wide, greens are huge, and the diameter of the hole is more than 2 1/2 times that of the ball.

Sure, there are trees, the rough, fences, and hazards, but you don't have to hit perfect golf shots to avoid them.

All you have to do is learn how to *control* your miss-hits. That's accomplished through adopting a more conservative approach to shot selection and developing a more efficient approach to shot making.

Poor shots hurt your score **more than good shots help your score.**

The important question is not how good your good shots are – it's how bad are your bad ones?
Harvey Penick

Poor shots are always penalizing because the next shot becomes more difficult – *often far more difficult* - than it would have been if you had merely hit an average shot.

It's also true that better than average shots make the next shot easier, but normally only slightly easier.

For example, let us say you're playing a 360-yard straight-a-way Par-4. The fairway is bordered by trees on the left and out-of-bounds on the right. The front of the green is guarded by a small pond and today the flag is located on the far right side of the green.

If you slice your tee shot out of bounds, you're going to have to replay your shot and take a one shot penalty. If you hook your tee shot into trees you're going to waste a shot pitching the ball back onto the fairway. If you significantly miss-hit your tee shot and it only travels a short distance, you'll have to lay up in front of the pond on your second shot. A bad hook, a bad slice, or a significant miss-hit will cost you *additional strokes*.

So what happens if you hit a better than average 250-yard drive in the center of the fairway - straighter and 20 yards farther than your normal drive? Do you get to take a stroke off your score? No, you're just 110 yards away from the green instead of your normal 130 yards – making your second shot *slightly* easier.

If you hit your second shot into the pond, it's going to cost you a one-stroke penalty to drop out. If you slice your second shot to the right of the green, you'll be left with a very difficult chip and probably bogey the hole because you'll have no green to work with. Again, a poor shot will either cost you *additional* strokes or make the next shot far more difficult than it should have been.

Let us say your normal second shot finishes on or around the green, about 40 feet from the hole. What happens if you hit a much better than average second shot onto the green - about 20 feet from the hole? Well, you're certainly closer to the hole than you normally are, but your chances of making the putt are quite small. In fact, you'll make that 20 foot putt less than one time in ten.

On this hole you could easily make par with your average 230-yard drive, an average second shot onto the green, and two average putts. You could also make an exceptional 250-yard drive, an exceptional second shot onto the green, a good putt that finishes next to the hole and tap in for your par. *But if you hit one or two poor shots there is no telling how high your score might be.*

The point being that poor shots hurt your score **far more than good shots help your score.**

I've seen many players break par without hitting one truly exceptional shot. You could make the lowest score in your life without hitting a single exceptional shot.

In his classic book *How to Play Your Best Golf All The Time*, the legendary Tommy Armour states, *"It is not solely the capacity to make great shots that make champions, but the essential quality of making very few bad shots."*

Categorize your shots into three groups:

Above Average Shots

Average Shots

Below Average Shots

Learning how to convert a good percentage of your *average shots* into *above average shots* would be very time consuming and extremely difficult. Furthermore, it will not lower your average score anywhere near the degree you believe it might.

On the other hand, learning how to convert a good percentage of your below average shots into average shots is much easier and will lower your average score far more than you realize.

I say it's *much easier* because it doesn't require endless practice. All you have to do is develop a more efficient approach to shot-making. In other words, become better at what is within your conscious control — *shot selection, club selection, intention, setup position and swing focus.*

As you develop a more efficient approach to shotmaking, you'll automatically reduce the number of poor shots you hit per round.

Lower scores are realized when you start replacing poor shots with average shots; which you can start doing immediately.

Lower scores stem from improved distance control, **but most golfers are only interested in hitting the ball farther.**

Hitting the ball pure and accurate is more rewarding than hitting it far. Don't forget that ever.
Moe Norman

Golf is a game of precision, not strength.
Jack Nicklaus

While the average golfer remains fixated on trying to hit the ball farther, the essence of good golf is *distance control* – not raw distance.

The long hitter who is unable to **control** his distances **has no advantage at all**.

The great Bobby Jones was one of the longest drivers in his era. Yet on approach shots he routinely used stronger lofted clubs and swung with less effort than his fellow competitors. Jones understood what most golfers seem to never learn – *the primary goal is to hit the ball the correct distance, what golf club you use is irrelevant.*

To improve your distance control, consider implementing the following 9 ideas:

1. Swing within yourself

As a general rule, golfers swing most efficiently with what they define as 80 to 85% effort. Above that, their swing starts to move off-balance and the quality of contact starts to diminish.

2. Play to your 85% distances

On the golf course, club selection should be based on swinging at 80 to 85% effort.

3. Allow for the slight miss-hit

Even when swinging at 80 to 85% effort, you're rarely going to make perfectly centered contact. Almost all of your shots are going to be a slight miss-hit and not carry quite as far as you might have anticipated. You have to allow for that and, when between clubs, it's normally better to error on the side of over-clubbing.

4. Try to calculate exact distances and results

When playing full shots on the golf course, before swinging, always try to calculate the *exact* carry distance to your target. Then, when you reach the green, check your ball mark and determine exactly how far you carried the shot. Soon you'll discover the average carry distance of every club in your bag.

5. On short shots, always think of distance first

On putts, chips and pitches there is minimal face rotation, so it's easy to hit the ball relatively straight. The primary concern on these shots should *always* be distance.

6. Consider replacing middle and long irons with hybrids and/or higher lofted fairway metals

With every golf club you should be able to create a high launching trajectory that produces a descending angle steep enough that the ball will hit and stay on the green. This is referred to as a *playable trajectory*. Lower trajectories are considered unmanageable because you have no control over how far the ball will travel once it hits the green.

If you're unable to achieve a playable trajectory with your middle or long irons, replace them with low center of gravity hybrids and/or higher lofted fairway metals – *clubs that are specifically designed to produce a higher launch angle.*

7. Check your yardage gaps

It serves no purpose to carry two or more clubs that you hit approximately the same distance. There should be at least a 8-yard (and preferably a 10 to 12-yard) playable carry distance between each club in your bag. To achieve this, you may have to alter your set composition.

8. Carry at least 3 clubs that you hit under 100 yards

Nothing influences your ability to score more than your short game distance control. You should play with at least three clubs that will carry less than 100-yards when swung with 80% effort. For example, a gap wedge that carries 95-yards, a sand wedge that carries 75-yards, and a lob wedge that carries 55-yards.

9. Become continually aware of clubface impact location

The key to distance control is a consistent quality of contact – *a consistent transfer of energy*. On every shot, strive to make contact in the center of the clubface. Become less concerned with clubhead speed and more concerned with the quality of contact.

Ben Hogan did not say golf was all about distance, he said that golf was all about management. **You cannot manage your game without distance control.**

In a round of golf, about 40% of your shots will be putts, **but few golfers truly appreciate the importance of putting.**

Putting has a bigger impact on scoring than most golfers are inclined to admit to themselves.
Jack Nicklaus

Golfers tend to find poor putting to be more acceptable than poor ball-striking. Maybe they consider a 3-putt to be less embarrassing than a poor drive. For whatever reason, they spend much more time on the driving range than the practice putting green. *That's unfortunate because improving your putting is not difficult and one of the quickest ways to lower your average score.*

There are four ways to **immediately improve your putting:**

1. Learn how to better read greens.

Learning how to effectively read the green is a learned skill that few golfers even try to acquire. *Regardless of the quality of your putting stroke, if you can't determine the line of the putt you're not going to make many putts.*

There is no reason to *over analyze* a putt, because there will always be inconsistencies on the putting surface that are beyond your ability to consider. But there is also no reason to not give every putt your *full consideration*. It doesn't take a lot of time or effort, just a trained eye.

In reading greens, golfers tend to make two critical mistakes. First, they usually underestimate the break – it has been estimated that amateur golfers miss close to 85% of their putts on the low side. Second, they give no consideration to how the grain of the grass will influence the speed of the putt.

2. Learn how to strike the ball squarely.

Golfers are generally so concerned with manipulating the back-and-forth motion of their putter head, they fail to consider the more important issue of face alignment at impact. ***The alignment of the putter face at impact influences launch direction far more than the path of the putter head.***

Two-time PGA champion and short game guru Paul Runyun once said, *"If there's a key to being a good putter it's having a deep understanding of how to hit the ball squarely."* Notice that he did not say "a deep understanding of the back-and-forth motion of the putter head", he said "a deep understanding of how to *hit the ball squarely*".

Bobby Jones said that he would visualize a tiny tack sticking out of the back of the ball, and when putting he would just drive the tack into the ball with the sweet spot of the putter face.

Square the putter face to your intended line and make it your primary intention to return it to that position at impact – *to hit the ball squarely.*

3. Focus more on distance control than the line of the break.

Golfers tend to consider the line of the putt far more than the distance. They should take the opposite approach. In putting (and every other aspect of golf) *distance control* is of primary importance.

You'll seldom miss-read the line of a putt by more than a foot, but you can easily miss-judge the distance of a putt by several feet. ***Always make distance your primary concern.***

4. Use a putter that compliments your setup position and stroke.

Today most large retailers offer a free custom fitting with the purchase of a new driver. It's a service most golfers have come to expect. Unfortunately, even if you were able to add a few yards to your average drive, it's not going to lower your average score. ***Becoming a better putter, however, produces lower scores immediately. Yet, golfers seldom get fit for their putter.***

The problem is that retailers generally don't offer a complimentary fitting with the purchase of a putter. They feel they can sell putters without providing that service. *Golfers are led to believe that a driver fitting is of great value, while a putter fitting isn't even necessary.*

Remember that retailers are in business to make money, **not lower handicaps.**

With a properly fit putter, after assuming your normal comfortable address position, the head of the putter will sit flat on the ground, directly under your eyes. From that viewpoint, it's easier to square the putter face, strike the putt squarely and get the ball rolling on your intended line.

You shouldn't have to adjust your posture to fit your putter. *You should adjust the specifications of the putter to fit your posture.* It's not difficult - you need only alter the shaft length and lie-angle. Any competent club maker can do it.

It's also easy to, if needed, adjust the loft of your putter. Putters are generally designed with 3 or 4 degrees of loft, which is adequate if you make contact with your hands *slightly ahead of the ball.* Unfortunately, not all golfers putt that way. If you strike the ball with your hands well ahead of the ball, you may need to add a few degrees of loft to your putter. If you strike the putt with your hands straight above or slightly behind the ball, you may have to slightly reduce the loft of your putter.

With a properly fit putter, it's easier to strike the ball squarely.

While continuously struggling to lower their average score, **golfers remain oblivious to the number of strokes they needlessly lose on the putting green.**

Most golfers hit very few greens in regulation, **but few golfers make an effort to improve their chipping, pitching, or sand shots.**

If you want to score, the most important 'game' to improve is your short game.

Dave Pelz

Poor chipping is the primary reason the handicap of the average golfer has remained frozen.

Corey Pavin

You are said to have hit the green *in regulation* when you hit the ball onto the green of a Par-3 in one shot, onto the green of a Par-4 in two shots, or onto the green of a Par-5 in three shots.

After having hit a green *in regulation,* you're allowed two putts for your par. If you don't hit the green in regulation, you'll very often need to substitute your first putt for a chip, pitch, or sand shot.

People think that professional golfers hit almost every green in regulation, but that's certainly not true. The average number of greens hit in regulation on the PGA Tour is around 12. For that reason, tour players work very hard on their chipping, pitching, and sand shots. If they don't, they know they're going make a lot of bogies and not much money. ***Research proves that the short game is the single greatest influence on the success or failure of a touring professional.***

The average golfer generally hits three or fewer greens in regulation, yet almost never practices shots around the green. **From a scoring perspective, this makes no sense at all.**

In his highly acclaimed book, *Dave Pelz's Short Game Bible,* Pelz writes, *"From ten feet no one consistently holes better than 25% of their putts. Your best chance of making a putt is if it's inside 10 feet. And how do you get there? Answer: the wedges, pitches, chips, and bunker shots of your short game."*

In a normal round of golf around 35% of your shots are going to be full swings. **Yet the average golfer only practices full swings.**

If the short game is 65% of your golf game, doesn't it deserve 65% of your practice time? Think of it this way, if your average score was 100, a 10% improvement in the short game would equate to 6.5 shots. On the other hand, a 10% improvement in your long game would only equate to 3.5 shots. ***Practicing your short game is the most efficient use of your practice time.***

Golf is about distance control. **Scoring is about short game distance control.**

The golfer determines how difficult the course will play, **and most golfers make the course more difficult than it really is.**

Golf is a game of percentages, I play percentages.
Byron Nelson

With poor shot selection you'll continually need to hit exceptional shots. First, you need to hit great shots to avoid hitting into penalizing situations. Then you'll need to hit great shots to get out of the difficult situations you'll find yourself continuously in.

The same course on the same day can be wide open and require only average shots or it can be very tight and require a series of precision shots.

You get to determine how the course will play **through shot selection.**

Off the tee, you can make it a priority to hit every drive as far as possible or you can make it a priority to keep the ball in the fairway. On approach shots, you can choose to always aim directly at the flag or you can choose to aim at the middle or safe side of the green.

The problem most golfers have is that they believe they hit the ball significantly farther and straighter than they actually do.

As a result, they take costly gambles, and continuously find themselves in undesirable situations.

The best golfers don't take those gambles. Renowned golf instructor Jim McLean writes, *"Jack Nicklaus played his entire career by hitting mostly to the center of the green...Amateurs go flag hunting a lot too often, and it severely hurts their scoring ability and enjoyment."*

Evaluating the risk-reward relationship on every shot was a major part of the Jack Nicklaus approach to course management. In his mind, he actually kept a ranking of where he didn't want the ball to go. That ranking in descending order of importance was:

Out of bounds
Where the ball could be lost
Unplayable zone
Water
Woods
Severe rough
Deep or high lipped bunker
Severely angled lie
Shallow bunker
Light rough
Slightly angled lie

He would reduce the possibility of hitting into any of those areas through – *as much as possible* - aiming away from them.

At first I thought it was odd that Nicklaus was so emphatic about where he *didn't* want the ball to go. It seemed negative. In truth, Nicklaus knew what few golfers ever learn – *that poor shots will hurt your score more than good shots will help your score.*

Furthermore, there was nothing at all negative about his approach. After determining where he didn't want to go, he'd choose his target and form *a very positive intention* to hit the ball to that exact spot.

Determining where he didn't want to go was nothing more than the first step in his process of selecting his ultimate target.

Regardless of your level of play, golf is a game of managing mishits. And the first step to managing mishits is to adopt a conservative approach to shot selection.

Jack Nicklaus writes, *"Before every shot – drive, approach, pitch, chip, putt – ask yourself, "I'm trying for a great play here, but what allowance should I make to 'protect my score' in case I don't make my very best swing?"*

The allowance almost all golfers should make is to aim exactly in the middle or safe-side of every fairway and green. Make it a habit to approach each shot in the same way Tiger Woods says he does - *expect the best and prepare for the worst.*

Ben Hogan revealed the reasoning behind his very conservative approach to shot selection when he wrote, *"Management, placing the ball in the right position for the next shot, is eighty percent of wining golf"*. For him, the objective of the **immediate shot** was always to make the **next shot** as easy as possible.

Your normal shot will always be a slight mishit. **You prepare for that through adopting a conservative approach to shot selection.**

PART THREE
UNDERSTANDING GOLF
CLUBS

There is an old saying, "It's a poor craftsman who blames his tools."

Kathy Whitworth

Golf clubs are not getting better, **and there will never be a golf club that perfectly fits your golf swing.**

Those are the same clubs I used last week.
Last week I'm shooting 80 this week 70.
Lee Trevino

Manufactures claim their golf clubs are *better* every year because the designs are superior and the components are more expensive.

Most golfers, however, define a *better* golf club as one which will *somehow* produce lower scores. With that definition, you'd have to conclude that golf clubs are not getting *better* at all. If each year the newest *high tech design* in golf clubs was able to save you just one stroke per round, you could improve through doing nothing more than buying new golf clubs. Every year your handicap would *automatically* drop by a stroke.

That obviously has never happened and never will happen. Even though golf clubs are redesigned each year, they will never again offer the average golfer a meaningful benefit in performance. This is because to produce a *legal* golf club, manufacturers have to stay within the strict guidelines set forth by the United States Golf Association (USGA) and The Royal & Ancient Golf Club of St. Andrews, Scotland (R&A). These two governing bodies of golf are highly committed to protecting the integrity of the game. They have no interest in softening their rules. ***They're not going to allow golf club designers to make the game easier than it was intended to be.***

You must accept that everything that can be done to **significantly** improve the performance of a golf club **has already been done.**

With regards to performance, golf clubs are as good as they are going to get. ***There will always be changes in golf club design, but those changes are market driven and primarily cosmetic.*** Just because golf clubs look different every year doesn't mean they're getting better. *If they didn't at least look different, golfers wouldn't keep buying them.* So if you've been waiting for some future advance in golf club design to dramatically improve the performance of your game, you can forget about it.

You also need to accept that, there will never be a golf club that will always perfectly fit your golf swing.

Today, large retailers almost always offer a complimentary fitting session with the purchase of an expensive set of irons or an expensive driver. That leads to the question, how do you perfectly fit a golf club to a golf swing that's always changing? **Obviously you can't; a golfer is not a mechanical golf machine, he's *human golf machine.***

If there was such a thing as perfectly fit golf clubs, don't you think the players on the PGA Tour would have them? And if you believe they do have them, explain to me why so many touring professionals continuously change their equipment.

Your swing changes slightly on a daily basis because your body and state of mind change slightly on a daily basis. *That's why a golf club that seems to perfectly fit your swing on one day may not work quite as well the next day.* **That is also why golf club fitting will never be an exact science.**

It would be nice if the retailer's *15-minute high-tech fitting process* could reveal a magic set of specifications that you could use to determine the *perfect* golf club, but it is never going to happen. A golf club with specifications that will perfectly fit your golf swing *everyday* doesn't exist – and will never exist.

That certainly does not mean that you should forget about being fit for your golf clubs; **it means that you should be realistic about your fitting objectives.**

Instead of continuously changing your golf clubs, **just get fit for a set of clubs that are easy for YOU to use.**

Some players are never satisfied unless they are buying new clubs ... This is not good for the player, but it is quite good for the clubmaker.

James Braid
Five-time British Open Champion between 1901 and 1910

There are golf club designs and specifications that complement your size, strength, and basic swing motion. With the help of a **qualified club fitter**, it's not difficult to assemble a set of 14 golf clubs that will be easy for you to use.

The person fitting you should have an in-depth knowledge of each of the three components of the golf club (*head, shaft, and grip*); and understand how to most effectively assemble your set (*assemble the appropriate combination of wedges, irons, hybrids and fairway metals*). He should also be able to fully explain the reasoning behind **each of his recommendations**. You should test his knowledge through asking questions similar to these:

Why do you recommend this particular grip and grip size?

57

How do you determine what style of iron head is best for me?

What advantages does an offset iron head provide?

How do you determine the correct lie angle for my irons?

How does the iron lie angle affect ball-flight?

Is fitting wedges different than fitting irons?

Will you also adjust the lie angle of the wedges I purchase?

What is the real difference between graphite and steel shafts?

Are expensive graphite shafts worth the money, and if so, why?

Why does shaft flex matter and what flex is best for me?

Why is the shaft bend profile different from shaft flex?

What is the best shaft bend profile for me?

How do you determine the correct shaft length for me?

Why do golfers replace some of their irons with hybrids?

How do you determine what would be the best combination of wedges, irons, hybrids, and fairway metals for me?

Why do some golfers use high-lofted fairway metals instead of hybrids?

Does every golfer need to play with a 3-wood?

How does the face angle of a fairway metal affect ball flight?

How do you determine the correct loft and face angle for my driver?

Why do some players benefit when switching to an offset driver?

Why would I need an adjustable driver?

Would I hit the ball farther with a more flexible driver shaft?

Would I hit the ball farther with a longer shaft?

How do you fit putters?

Why would a fit putter help me putt better?

A qualified club fitter will be able to answer these **very basic questions** quickly and confidently.

In the club fitting process, there are three fundamental objectives:

1. **Specifications** – the fitter needs to determine the specifications that will allow YOU to make **square and centered contact with a playable trajectory** the highest percentage of time. The **primary fitting specifications** are: **Grip** *size and type;* **Shaft** *length, weight, flex and bend profile;* **Head** *design, lie angle (irons), and face angle (woods).*

2. **Set Composition** – The fitter needs to determine the combination of wedges, irons, hybrids, and fairway metals that will work best for YOU. You should be able to **effectively play** *(achieve a playable trajectory)* with every club; and there should be an appropriate **gap in carry distance** *(at least 8 to 10 yards)* between each club in your bag.

   It serves no purpose to play with a golf club you can't get properly elevated, and it serves no purpose to carry two or more clubs that you hit essentially the same distance.

3. **Set Balance** – You have fourteen clubs in your bag. When you remove the putter and driver, each of the remaining twelve clubs will fall into one of four categories – *wedges, irons, hybrids or fairway metals.* In a balanced set, the specifications of each club will complement the other clubs in its category; and the specifications of each category will complement the remaining three.

As soon as you acquire a set of golf clubs that satisfy these three fundamental objectives, stop searching for new equipment. There comes a point where seeking to improve your ball-striking through further refining your equipment is a waste of time. With regards to lowering your average score, ***there are far more important things for you to consider.***

If you don't improve your playing skills, you will not lower your average score, **regardless of how often you change your equipment.**

PART FOUR
UNDERSTANDING BALL
FLIGHT

In my mind one acquired trait to becoming a good golfer stands out well ahead of all others. It is a total understanding of golfing cause and effect - a precise knowledge of exactly what is required in terms of club and ball impact to make a golf ball travel in a particular manner.

Jack Nicklaus

Your swing motion creates impact conditions, **and impact conditions create ball flight.**

Being able to identify the 'geometry' of impact from the flight of the ball is fundamental to playing golf up to your maximum potential.

John Jacobs

You can swing a golf club many different ways and create the same ball flight. **Therefore, ball flight cannot tell you how you swung.**

There is no mystery to why the ball flies the way it does, it's a matter of *cause and effect*. **The impact dynamics (cause) creates the ball flight (effect).**

The physics of exactly how impact dynamics create ball flight is complex. The ball is in contact with the clubface for *about* three-quarters of an inch and *around* 5/10,000th of a second. To determine *exactly* how the ball will fly after leaving the clubface, you would have to determine *exactly* what was happening during that 5/10,000th of a second.

You would have to consider the speed of the clubhead, the orientation of the clubface, the impact location on the clubface, the design of the clubface, the design of the clubhead, the exact line on which the clubhead is traveling, and the physical characteristics of the golf ball.

Fortunately, you don't have to be a mechanical engineer to play great golf. In fact, as Bobby Jones put it, *"Anyone who hopes to reduce putting – or any other department of the game of golf for that matter – to an exact science, is in for a serious disappointment, and will only suffer from the attempt."*

It is, however, important for a golfer to understand impact dynamics in a *practical way*. **In the practical way a good pool player understands how a cue ball needs to be struck to create a particular shot.**

A good pool player does not focus on the movement of his arm, he focuses on striking the ball with the tip of his cue stick in a particular manner. Similarly, instead of focusing on the movements of his body, a golfer should focus on striking the ball with the face of his golf club in a particular manner.

From this point on, when you see ball flight, think of the impact conditions that actually *created it,* **not of the swing motion *associated with it.***

Always associate ball flight with impact conditions, **not swing motion.**

Launch direction is determined primarily **by the aim of the clubface at impact.**

The direction in which the clubface looks is the most important of the four impact elements that determine the behavior of every shot you hit.

John Jacobs

For years it was taught that the ball would always launch *in the direction the clubhead was traveling at impact.* You were led to believe that regardless of what shot you were playing (putt, chip, pitch, or full swing) if you swung the clubhead toward the target, the ball would always launch toward the target. And if the ball happened to launch to the left or right of the target, it was always because you swung the clubhead on a line aimed to the left or right of the target.

While that is very easy to understand, it's not true. *Launch direction is determined primarily by the aim of the clubface at impact.*

This can easily be demonstrated on the putting green. Find a level three foot putt; then hit three short putts, *each time swinging the clubhead straight down the target line.* Stroke the first putt with the putter face aimed at the center of the hole. Stroke the second putt with the clubface aimed slightly to the right of the hole. And stroke the third putt with the clubface aimed slightly to the left of the hole.

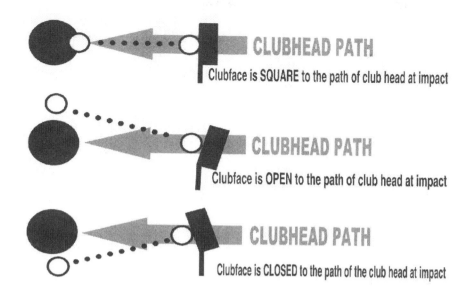

CLUBHEAD PATH

Clubface is SQUARE to the path of club head at impact

CLUBHEAD PATH

Clubface is OPEN to the path of club head at impact

CLUBHEAD PATH

Clubface is CLOSED to the path of the club head at impact

Notice that the ball always responds to the aim of the clubface at impact - **not the path of the clubhead.**

When the clubface is perpendicular to the path of the clubhead, it is said to be **SQUARE** *TO THE PATH*. From the perspective of a right handed golfer, when the clubface is aimed to the *RIGHT* of the path of the clubhead, it is said to be **OPEN** *TO THE PATH*. And when the clubface is aimed to the *LEFT* of the path of the clubhead it is said to be **CLOSED** *TO THE PATH*.

Again, from the perspective of a right handed golfer, any shot launched to the *RIGHT* of the target line is referred to as a **PUSH** and any shot launched to the *LEFT* of the target line is referred to as a **PULL**.

As you can see from the illustrations on the previous page, *pulls* and *pushes* are created primarily by the aim of the clubface at impact, **not the path of the clubhead.**

To further prove this point, stroke two more putts, this time keeping the clubface aimed at the center of the hole. On the first putt swing the clubhead on a line aimed slightly to the right of the hole – on a path described as ***INSIDE-to-OUTSIDE.*** On the second putt swing the clubhead on a line aimed slightly to the left of the hole – on a path described as ***OUTSIDE-to-INSIDE.***

Notice that the ball will still go into the hole if the putter face *is* ***aimed directly at the center of the hole at impact.***

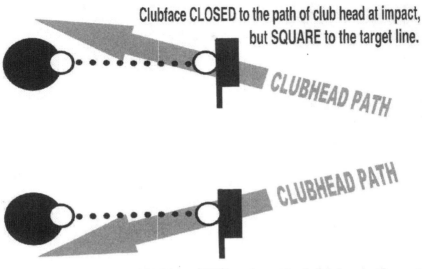

The truth is that on a dead-straight five-foot putt, you could swing your putter head on a line aimed a foot right or left of the hole center and still make the putt if at impact the putter face was aimed at the center of the hole and contact was square and centered.

The path of the clubhead will certainly influence launch direction, **but only to a limited degree.** The exact degree is relative to the speed of the clubhead and loft of the clubface at impact.

From a practical perspective, regardless of what club is being used, **the golfer need only associate launch direction with the aim of the clubface at impact.**

In-flight curvature occurs when the clubface is not **square to the path of the clubhead at impact.**

The ultimate judge of your swing is the flight of the ball.
BEN HOGAN

The golf ball does not launch off the clubface with both BACKSPIN and SIDESPIN because **the ball cannot spin in two directions at the same time.**

The golf ball flies through the air, spinning backward on a *SINGLE AXIS OF ROTATION* that is commonly referred to as the **SPIN AXIS.**

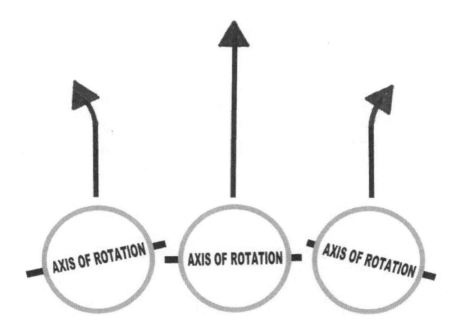

If the **SPIN AXIS** is horizontal (level to the ground), the golf ball will fly in a straight line. If the **SPIN AXIS** is tilted to the right, the golf ball will curve to the right. If the **SPIN AXIS** is tilted to the left, the golf ball will curve to the left.

How the *SPIN AXIS* is tilted is determined by the aim of the clubface ***relative to the path of the clubhead at impact.*** At impact, the clubface will either be *SQUARE, OPEN,* or *CLOSED* to the path of the clubhead.

While in contact with the lofted clubface, the ball compresses (flattens out) and *starts* to slide/roll upward before quickly rebounding to its original shape and launching forward. *It's because of this* **slight upward roll** *that the ball launches off the clubface with backspin.*

If at impact, the clubface is square to the path of the clubhead, the ball will start to roll **straight up the clubface** and launch forward spinning around a level (horizontal) spin axis. But if the clubface is angled to the path of the clubhead, the ball will start to roll **up the clubface on that angle** and launch forward spinning around an angled spin axis.

The ball will fly on a straight line when at impact *the clubface is square to the path of the clubhead (as illustrated below)*.

Clubface square to path of club head

When at impact the clubface is square to the path of the clubhead, *CONTACT IS MADE DIRECTLY TO THE BACK OF THE BALL*, and the ball will start to roll *straight up the clubface*. As a result, the ball will launch spinning backward on a level *HORIZONTAL SPIN AXIS* and fly in a straight line.

The ball will launch in the direction the clubface is aimed (which may or may not be at the target) and fly in a straight line because of the level *HORIZONTAL SPIN AXIS*.

The ball will hook when at impact *the clubface is closed to the path of the clubhead (as illustrated below)*.

Clubface closed to path of club head

When at impact the clubface is closed to the path of the clubhead, *CONTACT IS MADE TOWARD THE OUTSIDE OF THE BALL*, *causing the ball's upward roll to be angled toward the heel-side of the clubface.* As a result, the ball will launch spinning backward on a *SPIN AXIS* tilted slightly to the left, causing the ball to curve to the left (hook) as it decelerates.

The ball launches in the direction the clubface is pointing and then curves to the **LEFT** because the **SPIN AXIS IS TILTED TO THE LEFT.**

The ball will slice when at impact **the clubface is open to the path of the clubhead.**

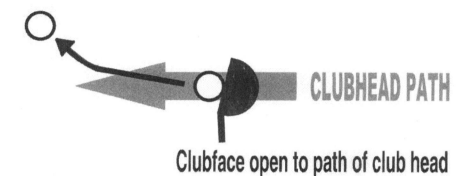

Clubface open to path of club head

When at impact the clubface is open to the path of the clubhead, **CONTACT IS MADE ON THE INSIDE OF THE BALL**, *causing the ball's upward roll to be angled toward the toe-side of the clubface.* As a result, the ball will launch spinning backward on a **SPIN AXIS** tilted slightly to the right, causing the ball to curve to the right (slice) as it decelerates.

The ball launches in the direction the clubface is pointing and then curves to the **RIGHT** because the **SPIN AXIS IS TILTED TO THE RIGHT.**

The angular difference between the **PATH OF THE Clubhead** and the **AIM OF THE CLUBFACE** is referred to as the **DIFFEREN-TIAL.** The greater the *DIFFERENTIAL,* **the more the ball will hook or slice.**

When the ball slices, you know the clubface was open to the path of the clubhead at impact.

When the ball hooks, **you know the clubface was closed to the path of the clubhead at impact.** When the ball flies in a straight line, **you know the clubface was square to the path of the clubhead at impact.**

Where you strike the ball on the clubface **will greatly influence how far the ball will fly.**

There are really two ways to increase your distance. You can learn to swing the clubhead faster. Or you can learn to deliver it to the ball more accurately.

Jack Nicklaus

If you don't make contact in the center of the clubface *(in-line with the clubhead's center of gravity)*, the clubhead will twist at impact, and the ball will travel off-line and a shorter distance than anticipated.

Most golfers believe the shaft will prevent the clubhead from twisting at impact, **but that's not true.**

The shaft delivers the clubhead to the ball, it does not stabilize the clubhead at impact. *In fact, the clubhead responds to impact as though it was not even connected to the shaft.* In Alister Cochrain's classic work *The Search for the Perfect Swing*, it is written, *"The clubhead responds to impact as though it were traveling through space alone, independent of the shaft".* **Remember, the ball is only in contact with the clubface for about 5/10,000th of a second and around three quarters of an inch.**

The speed of the clubhead and the impact location on the clubface will determine how much energy is transferred to the ball. ***You'll carry the ball farther with added clubhead speed, only if you're able to maintain square and centered contact.***

For example, with a driver, one mile-per-hour of clubhead speed equates to *almost* three yards of carry distance; *but only if the golfer is able to make square and centered contact.* All things being equal, a golfer who swings his driver head at 90 miles-per hour has the potential to carry his drives *almost* 15 yards farther than a golfer with 85 mile-per-hour head speed. But, if he misses the center of the clubface, the clubhead will turn at impact and less energy will be transferred to the ball.

In his book, *Golf Club Fitting & Performance,* legendary golf club designer *Ralph Maltby* estimates that with a driver if you make contact with the ball one inch to the left or right of the center of the clubface will lose *about* 14% of your carry distance. ***In other words, the drive that you would have carried 250 yards if you had made square and center contact, will only carry around 215 yards, if you happen to miss the center of the clubface by an inch!***

Furthermore, the further from the center of the clubface contact is made, **the more distance will be lost.** This applies to every golf shot – putter through driver. When you don't make contact in the center of the clubface, the clubhead turns at impact, less energy is transferred to the ball, and you lose distance.

This is also why sometimes you hit the ball farther when you swing slower; ***the quality of contact is better.***

Learning how to make square and centered contact a higher percentage of time **is far more important than learning how to increase your clubhead speed.**

How you deliver the clubface to the ball **will greatly influence how high the ball will fly.**

Trajectory is the key to shotmaking.
BEN HOGAN

Some golfers hit high-lofted drivers very low and some golfers hit low-lofted drivers very high. That's because how you deliver the clubhead to the ball can influence launch trajectory *more than the loft of the clubhead*.

The loft on your driver is measured with the head sitting flat on the ground. It's referred to as the *STATIC LOFT.* To maintain that loft at impact, the sole of the driver head would have to be traveling parallel to the ground. That, however, is seldom the case.

Generally at impact the clubhead is either moving slightly upward or **(most often)** slightly downward.

The degree in which the clubhead is moving upward or downward at impact is referred to as the *ANGLE OF APPROACH.*

The loft of the driver **at impact** is known as the **EFFECTIVE LOFT**. When the clubhead is moving upward the *effective loft* is *increased* and the ball is launched at a higher angle. When the clubhead is moving downward the *effective loft* is *decreased* and the ball is launched at a lower angle.

You'll notice the same effect when hitting iron shots. Let's say you normally position the ball in the middle of your stance when hitting a 7-iron. As you move the ball back in your stance (toward the right foot for a right-handed golfer) you will tend to strike the ball with a more descending blow, *decrease the effective loft*, and launch the ball lower. Conversely, as you move the ball forward in your stance (toward the left foot for a right-handed golfer) you'll tend to strike the ball with less of a descending blow, *increase the effective loft*, and launch the ball higher.

The effective loft is also influenced by **the alignment of the clubface at impact.**

When the clubface is rolled to an **OPEN POSITION** the effective loft is increased and when the clubface is rolled to a **CLOSED POSITION** the effective loft is decreased.

This is easily demonstrated on chip shots. From a few yards off the green, hit three chips with your pitching wedge, **each time swinging the clubhead straight down the target line**. Hit the first chip with the clubface **SQUARE** to the target line (aimed directly at the target). Hit the second chip with the clubface **CLOSED** to the target line (aimed significantly to the left of the target). And hit the third chip with the clubface **OPEN** to the target line (aimed significantly to the right of the target).

When you make contact in the middle of the clubface, with the clubface SQUARE to the target line, **the ball will fly at a normal pitching wedge trajectory and roll a predictable distance straight toward the target**.

When you roll the clubface to a **CLOSED POSITION** you, in effect, turn your wedge into a 9 or 8-iron. As a result, the ball will launch to the left of the target line (where the clubface is aimed), fly lower than normal and roll farther than anticipated (due to the lower loft).

When you roll the clubface to an **OPEN POSITION** you, in effect, turn your pitching wedge into a gap wedge or sand wedge. As a result, the ball will launch to the right of the target line (where the clubface is aimed) fly higher than normal and roll shorter than anticipated (due to the higher loft).

You'll realize the same results **when making a full swing.**

When the clubface is in an **OPEN POSITION** at impact, the ball will launch to the right, fly higher and travel shorter than expected. When the clubface is in a **CLOSED POSITION** at impact, the ball will launch to the left, fly lower and travel longer than expected. *This is why hooking shots tend to travel lower and longer than slicing shots.*

The launch angle is determined by the loft of the golf club and, more importantly, **by how you deliver the clubface to the ball.**

Backspin is created primarily by **effective loft and clubhead speed.**

It is not true, though – and this goes against much long-established lore of golf – that the rougher the surface of the club the more backspin it will necessarily impart on the ball.

Alastair Cochran
Search for the Perfect golf Swing

A golf club does not hit a golf ball *squarely* in the same sense that a hammer hits a nail *squarely* into a wall. That's because all golf clubs have loft and are designed to make contact with the golf ball in an *oblique* manner.

Regardless of what club you're using, when the ball is properly struck with a lofted clubface **it will launch forward with some degree of backspin.**

You don't need to purchase an expensive golf club with a ***specially designed clubface*** to create added backspin.

Added backspin is created primarily by **increasing the effective loft** and **clubhead speed.**

For example, at a normal 8-iron distance from your target, if you need added backspin you might choose to hit a 9-iron (more loft) and swing the clubhead faster than normal (more clubhead speed). *The result will be a higher-flying shot with greater backspin.*

There are times, however, when you need to hit an approach shot with *less* backspin. When hitting into the wind, for example. This is accomplished through taking the exact opposite approach. From a normal 8-iron distance you might choose to hit a 6 or 7-iron (less loft), choke down on the club and swing easier than normal (creating less clubhead speed). *The result will be a low-flying shot with less than normal backspin.*

Most golfers believe that you can *greatly* increase backspin with the same golf club through simply applying a more descending blow. ***That, however, is not exactly true.***

A more descending blow will certainly add backspin; but it also reduces the effective loft, which *reduces* backspin. Hitting more down on the ball with the same golf club and same swing speed lowers the launch angle but does not *significantly* influence the rate of spin.

Having said this, it is still VERY IMPORTANT ***to hit down on the ball with your irons and wedges***. You need a descending blow to minimize the amount of debris (*grass, water, dirt*) caught between the ball and clubface at impact.

To create backspin, you need friction between the ball and clubface; **you need clean contact.**

Without friction, the ball tends to ***slide*** up the clubface more than ***roll*** up the clubface. Debris acts as a lubricant and diminishes friction. *This is why it is so difficult to spin the ball when hitting out of the rough; at impact there is debris between the ball and the clubface.*

This is also why the grooves are so important; **they perform a function similar to the tread on your tires**

In wet conditions, the treads on your tires channel away surface moisture, so the tire stays in contact with the surface of the road; they prevent "hydroplaning".

The grooves on the clubface act in a similar fashion. At impact, grass, water and dirt are smashed into the grooves, allowing for an increased degree of contact between the ball and clubface; thus *more friction* and added backspin.

The larger the volume of the grooves, the more debris they can accommodate, and the easier it becomes to spin the ball out of the rough.

Average golfers often lose backspin around the green because they both **decelerate the clubhead** and **reduce the effective loft**.

When you decelerate you lose clubhead speed, and when you allow the clubhead to roll to a *closed position* you lose loft. If you watch professionals hit a chip, pitch or lob shots you'll notice they always accelerate through impact and keep the clubface square to the target line until well after the ball has been launched. Some maintain their square impact position to the finish of their swing motion.

There are times, however, when you need **less backspin** on a short shot.

For example, when you're chipping the ball across a large green and want the ball to roll the majority of the way to the hole. You can launch the ball with less backspin through merely using a lower lofted golf club; *possibly a 7-iron instead of a pitching wedge*. The reduced loft will allow you to hit the ball the required distance with less clubhead speed. *Reduced loft and less clubhead speed produces less backspin and, therefore, more roll.*

Finally, it's easier to launch the ball with added backspin when you play with a golf ball **specifically designed to produce added backspin.**

Many of the high-spin approach shots you watch touring professionals hit on television would be impossible with an inexpensive hard covered 2-piece golf ball. If you're seriously intent on *maximizing* backspin, you're going to have to play with a soft covered, multilayered golf ball.

You need to remember, however, that these balls don't spin themselves. ***They need to be struck cleanly and squarely with significant loft and clubhead speed.*** Unfortunately, most golfers don't have the skill needed to take advantage of the benefits these (expensive) golf balls offer.

You can significantly increase or decrease the amount of backspin imparted onto the ball through significantly increasing or decreasing the **effective loft, the clubhead speed, or both.**

Questions about ball flight that serious golfers **should be able to easily answer.**

Now that you've acquired a practical understanding of impact dynamics, see if you can apply what you've learned to answer the following questions. **All the questions are answered from the perspective of a right-handed golfer.**

1. Why does my 7-iron fly farther when I hook it and shorter when I slice it?

When you hook the ball, the face is *closed to the path of the clubhead.* When you *close* the clubface you reduce the *effective loft* – causing the ball to fly lower, longer, and with reduced backspin. *Your 7-iron plays more like a 6-iron.*

When you slice the ball, the face is *open to the path of the clubhead.* When you *open* the clubface you increase the *effective loft* – causing the ball to fly higher, shorter, and with added backspin. *Your 7-iron plays more like an 8-iron.*

2. Why do my long irons slice more than my short irons?

Because short irons have more loft, their clubface contacts the ball significantly below the ball's equator. This promotes added backspin and the **spin axis** tends to stay relatively level, *regardless of the alignment of the clubface.*

Because long irons have less loft, contact is made closer to the ball's equator. As a result, there is less backspin and it becomes far easier for an open clubface to **tilt the spin axis**.

This is why a 3-iron struck with a 2-degree open clubface will slice considerably farther to the right than a 9-iron struck with a 2-degree open clubface.

It is also why players hit high lofted drivers more accurately than they hit low lofted drivers. The added **effective loft** keeps the ball's **spin axis** closer to horizontal.

3. Why do some golfers hit low-lofted drivers very high, while other golfers hit high-lofted drivers very low?

It's because golfers deliver the clubhead to the ball quite differently.

When you strike the ball with either a **descending blow** or **closed clubface**, you reduce the loft and therefore decrease the launch angle. Conversely, when you strike the ball with either an **ascending blow** or **open clubface,** you **increase the effective loft** and therefore increase the launch angle.

4. I don't hit the ball as far as I used to, does that mean I've lost clubhead speed?

A sudden loss in distance is almost always related to the quality of contact, not a loss of clubhead speed.

Check the ***impact location*** on your clubface. When you make contact away from the center of the clubface, the clubhead turns at impact, less energy is transferred to the ball, and you lose substantial carry distance. ***The farther from center you make contact, the more distance you lose.***

5. My divot was pointing to the left side of the green, but my ball started off to the right side of the green and sliced further right. How could that happen?

Remember, your ball launches in the direction the clubface is aimed at impact. In this example, your clubhead was traveling on a line to the left side of the green (*we know that by looking at the divot*), but your clubface was aimed to the right side of the green (*we know that because the ball launched toward the right side of the green*). Because the clubface was significantly ***open to the path of the clubhead***, the ***spin axis*** was significantly ***tilted to the right,*** causing the ball to slice further to the right.

6. My divot was aiming directly at the flag, but my ball started off to the left and hooked further left. What happened?

At impact, your clubhead was traveling straight down the target line, but your clubface was ***closed to the path of the clubhead***. That's why the ball started to the left (where the clubface was aimed) and hooked further left (due to the ***tilt of the spin axis*** created because the clubface was not square to the path of the clubhead).

7. Will I be able to spin the ball more if I keep my clubface clean?

Yes. When your clubface is dirty there'll be debris between the ball and clubface at impact. The debris acts as a lubricant. It reduces the friction between the ball and the clubface and therefore reduces the degree of backspin. Also, when the grooves are filled with debris, the club becomes less effective out of the rough. ***Keeping your clubface and grooves clean will promote added backspin.***

8. My ball usually starts off to the left and then slices back to the right. But sometimes my ball starts off way left and doesn't slice back. Why not?

In this example, your clubhead is traveling to the left of the target on an ***outside-to-inside path***. When you **square** your clubface to this **path** your ball goes straight left (referred to as a **straight pull**). When you **open** the clubface to this **path**, the ball will slice back toward your target (referred to as a ***pull slice***). *The more the clubface is **open to the path**, the more the ball will launch toward the target line and the more it will slice to the right.*

9. When playing into the wind, I should hit the ball at a lower trajectory with less backspin. How do I do that?

When playing into the wind, most golfers select a club with *too much loft*, position the ball *back in their stance*, and strike the ball with a *hard descending blow*. This technique produces a low launching shot with a ***great deal of backspin.*** Because the wind amplifies spin, these golfers often find their ball ballooning upward or curving significantly off-line.

You can create the same trajectory with far less spin through selecting a *lower lofted club*, playing the ball from your *normal ball position*, and striking the ball with an *easier sweeping blow.* If you're afraid you'll hit the ball too far, just choke down on the shaft and swing even easier. ***Remember that lower clubhead speed produces less spin.***

10. Should I move the ball forward in my stance to hit the ball higher and back in my stance to hit the ball lower?

Trajectory is determined primarily by **effective loft** (loft of the clubface at impact). Moving the ball forward or backward in your stance certainly influences the effective loft, but it influences other factors into play as well.

Moving the ball forward in your stance can easily produce a **pull hook,** because at impact the clubface will tend to be **closing** and the clubhead will tend to be traveling on a line aimed to the left of the target.

Conversely, moving the ball back in your stance can easily produce a **push slice,** because at impact the clubface will tend to still be **open** and the clubhead will tend to be traveling on a line aimed to the right of the target.

You can certainly alter your trajectory through simply adjusting your ball position, many good golfers do; but you may also need to make adjustments to your grip and/or shoulder alignment to guard against the possibility of a **pull hook** or **push slice**.

The best way to make slight adjustments to your trajectory is through selecting a higher or lower lofted club and playing the ball from its normal position. For a slightly lower trajectory, select the next lower lofted club, choke down on the shaft, and shorten your swing. For a slightly higher trajectory select the next higher lofted club and make a fuller swing.

11. What should I do if I need to hit the ball high AND significantly farther?

In extreme situations, you'll need to adjust both your ball position and the alignment of your clubface. Let us say you have to carry the ball 140 yards over a tree that requires a 9-iron trajectory. If your maximum controllable carry distance with a 9-iron is 130 yards, what would you do?

To increase your clubhead speed, you'll need to select a club with a longer shaft, possibly a 7-iron. Then, to increase the *effective loft,* you'll need to position the ball forward in your stance, open the clubface and align yourself to the left of your target. From this set up position, the easiest shot to create would be a high fade. If your normal 7-iron carry distance was 150 yards, your high fade 7-iron should carry closer to 140 yards.

12. Is there an easy way to intentionally fade or draw the ball?

Yes, set up to the ball in the manner that makes it easy.

If you intended to *fade* the ball to your target, you would aim the clubface to the left of the target on the line you wanted the ball to launch – refer to this line as your *aim-line.* Then you align your feet and shoulders significantly to the left of your aim-line and *re-grip* the club. *The clubface will now appear to be open (aligned to the right), because it remains square to your aim-line.* From this position, you merely swing the clubhead in the direction your shoulders are pointing (well to the left of your aim-line). If all goes well, the ball will launch to the left of your target (in the direction the clubface was aimed at address) and fade to the right (because, at impact, the clubface will be *open to the path of the clubhead*).

To draw the ball to your target, you set up to the ball in the exact opposite manner. Establish an *aim-line* to the right of your target and square your clubface to that line. Then align your feet and shoulders further to the right and *re-grip* the club. *The clubface will now appear to be closed (aligned to the left), because it remains square to your aim-line.* From this position, you swing the clubhead in the direction your shoulders are pointing (well to the right of your aim-line). If all goes well, the ball will launch to the right of your target (in the direction the clubface was aimed at address) and draw to the left (because, at impact, the clubface will be *closed to the path of the clubhead).*

13. How can I get more backspin on my pitch shots?

Added backspin is created primarily by *added loft* and *added clubhead speed.*

To insure added loft, use a higher lofted club and don't allow the clubface to *close* until after the ball is launched. Remember, when you *close* the clubface you create *less effective loft* and therefore less spin.

If you're swinging the clubhead down the target line, but the ball is launching to the left of your target line, it's because the clubface is *closed at impact*. As a result, the ball will launch lower and roll farther.

To insure added clubhead speed, always accelerate through impact.

Once you learn how to consistently create the pitch shot impact conditions that produce added backspin (*square clubface* with *significant effective loft* and *clubhead speed)*, you can create even more backspin through switching to a soft covered multi-layered golf ball.

14. I always miss my short putts to the left. Does this mean I'm swinging the putter head across my target line from outside-to-inside?

Not necessarily.

Remember, the ball will launch in the direction the putter face is aimed at impact. You could be swinging the clubhead straight down the target line, but if the putter face is *closed* (aimed to the left) the ball will always launch to the left. And if the clubface is *open* (aimed to the right) the ball will always launch to the right.

If you were able to fully understand the answers to these 14 questions, congratulations. **You now know more about impact dynamics than 99% of all golfers!**

PART FIVE
UNDERSTANDING THE
GOLF SWING

…the object is not to swing in a specific manner, nor to execute a series of complicated movements in a prescribed sequence, not to look pretty while doing it, but primarily and essentially to strike the ball with the head of the club so that the ball will perform according to one's wishes.

Bobby Jones

A consistent swing motion stems from consistency in the set up position.

Most golfers ruin many of their shots before they even begin to swing, simply because they set themselves to the task in the wrong way. It really is absurd for an intelligent person to make no effort to get things right from the start.

John Jacobs

If you set up correctly, there's a good chance you'll hit a reasonable shot, even if you make a mediocre swing. If you set up incorrectly, you'll hit a lousy shot even if you make the greatest swing in the world.

Jack Nicklaus

Jack Nicklaus has always contended that forty to fifty percent of what it takes to hit a good golf shot is related to the set up position.

Peter Thompson, the legendary Australian golfer who won five British Opens went even further when he wrote that everything you needed to know about the golf swing technique could be written on two sheets of paper, and that 90 percent would deal with *getting set up right*.

Let me explain why that might be true.

Where you position the ball in your stance will affect the path of the clubhead, the angle of approach and the alignment of the clubface at impact.

Your grip pressure and how your align you hands on the grip will affect the alignment of the clubface at impact.

The width of your stance will affect your balance as well as your ability to turn in both directions.

The tension in your body will affect the length of your swing, as well as your tempo, rhythm and balance.

How you align your shoulders at address will influence the path of the clubhead at impact.

How you position your feet will affect your ability to turn in both directions, your swing plane, and the path of the clubhead at impact.

How far you stand from the ball will affect your swing plane and face impact location.

Your balance at address will affect your ability to maintain your balance while swinging.

Your posture at address will affect your balance and swing plane.

Arnold Palmer summed it up perfectly when he wrote, *"The golf swing is guided by and moves around the set up position".*

Unfortunately, there is no single best way for everyone to grip the club and setup to the ball. Just as everyone has a different swing motion, everyone should have a slightly different grip and set up position. This is what Harvey Penick was referring to when he wrote, *"You only need a perfect grip if you have a perfect swing".*

In his book, *The Full Swing,* Jack Nicklaus writes, *"In the long haul your forward swing will only be as good as your backswing. In turn, your backswing will only be as good as your preswing preparation."*

When your set up position changes, your swing motion will change. **It has to change.**

93

It doesn't matter how you swing, **so don't waste your time trying to swing exactly like someone else.**

If a great golf swing put you high on the money list, many of us would be broke.

Raymond Floyd
PGA, Masters, and US Open Champion

Legendary golf instructor John Jacobs states, *"The only object of the golf swing is to present the club correctly to the ball."* **If you look at the swings of the top 100 players in the world, you'll find that each player uses a different method to "present the club correctly to the ball".**

The fact that the top 100 players in the world all have noticeably different golf swings, should tell you something.

It should tell you that **how you swing** is not nearly as important as you've been led to believe.

It seems illogical that there are so many ways to successfully swing a golf club, but it's true. As John Jacobs further states, *"One reason I have always thought that golf can be such a difficult game is that there are so many ways to play it correctly."*

While lesser players hope to improve through copying the styles of others, the best players in the world have no problem being different. They'll employ any technique that improves the consistency of their ball-striking. ***Trying to look like someone else is not even a consideration.***

Lee Trevino

Early in his career, Lee Trevino battled a chronic hook. To solve the problem he developed his own *anti-hook* golf swing that looked like nothing anyone had ever seen. With a wide stance and strong grip, Trevino aimed far to the left of his target. On the backswing he swung the club back to the outside of his target line. On the forward swing he made a lateral shift, rerouted his arms back onto the proper swing plane, and held on tightly with his left hand through the hitting area. The result was a highly controllable slight fade. Because his swing motion was so unusual, many *experts* felt that it would not holdup under pressure and that Lee Trevino would be just another a splash in the pan. ***Trevino kept his swing and went on to win 2 US Opens, 2 British Opens, 2 PGA Championships, 23 other tournaments on the PGA Tour, and 29 tournaments on the Champions Tour. Today, he is universally recognized as one of the greatest ball strikers of all time.***

Charlie Owens

Competing on the 1986 Senior PGA Tour, Charlie Owens won twice and finished the year eighth on the money list with $207,813 in earnings. What is remarkable is that he played cross-handed with a fused left knee! ***Completely self-taught, Charlie claims to have never owned his own set of golf clubs until he was 37 years old.***

Calvin Peete

Living in poverty, at the age of 11, Calvin Peete fell out of a tree and broke his left elbow in 3 places. Unable to have his arm properly set, he was left permanently impaired. He didn't start playing golf until his mid 20s. Because of his late start and badly impaired left arm, he was given no chance to succeed as a professional golfer. Believing in himself and without ever taking a lesson, he worked diligently on developing his own swing and his own game. Limited in his ability to generate clubhead speed, he worked for years to develop his accuracy. Incredibly, at the age of 32, he qualified for the PGA Tour. *With his badly impaired left arm and self-taught swing, Calvin Peete went on to win 12 times on the PGA Tour and led the Tour in driving accuracy for an amazing 10 consecutive years, from 1981 to 1990.*

Allen Doyle

Growing up an avid hockey player, Allen Doyle believed that he could learn to play golf with a swing similar to that of the slap shot he used when playing hockey. With a wide stance and very little backswing, he appears to sweep the ball forward with every swing. After a brilliant amateur career, Doyle turned professional at the age of 46 and became the oldest player in history to qualify for the PGA Tour. *With his never seen before hockey style swing, he competed successfully on the Nike Tour, PGA Tour, and PGA Champions Tour. He won 11 times on the Champions Tour, including the 2005 and 2006 US Senior Opens.*

Ed Furgol

At the age of 12, Ed Furgol shattered his left elbow in a playground fall. He was left with a crooked, cocked left arm 10 inches shorter than his right arm. Desiring to become a professional golfer, Ed worked tirelessly on developing a swing motion than would overcome his physical deformity. *With his self-taught swing, Ed Furgol became a PGA Tour professional and won 6 times on the PGA Tour – including the 1954 US Open!*

Bernard Langer

Through most of his career, Bernard Langer struggled with a paralyzing fear of short putts. Numerous times his career was thought to be over due to his poor putting, but every time he fought back. Whenever the fears returned, he'd simply developed a radically different approach to putting. He invented putting grips and styles no one else had even tried. At one point, he used a cross-handed grip in which his left hand was extended far down the shaft and his right hand was used to clamp the putter grip against his left forearm. *Amazingly, while continuously changing his method of putting, he won 80 professional tournaments around the world, including 2 Masters – a tournament considered by many to be the world's most demanding putting contest.*

John Daly

John Daly has an incredibly long backswing and plays with a fast and highly aggressive style he refers to as "Grip it and rip it". As an amateur he was repeatedly told that he would have to develop a *shorter and more controllable* golf swing to achieve "any success at all" as a professional. *He kept his swing and went on to win the PGA Championship, the British Open, and almost ten million dollars on the PGA Tour*

Tim Clark

When Tim Clark won THE PLAYERS Championship in 2010, not many of his fellow competitors were surprised. Despite his small stature and lack of distance off the tee, he had been competing very successfully as a professional golfer for several years. What most fans didn't know is that Tim Clark suffers from a rare congenital condition that prevents him from rotating his arms so that his palms face upward. Because of that condition, he is unable to swing the golf club in the traditional manner and he is limited to the number of shots he can play around the green. *Instead of giving in to his physical limitations, Tim became his own coach, developed his own game, and has currently won over seventeen million dollars on the PGA Tour.*

Moe Norman

It is believed that Moe Norman developed autism as the result of a traumatic brain injury as a child. Suffering from severe shyness and a reclusive personality, Moe spent his teenage years alone, trying to learn how to hit a golf ball perfectly straight. Having never taken a golf lesson, Moe just developed his own swing through trial and error, and years of relentless practice. He kept his legs very straight, his stance was very wide, and he swung flat footed. He gripped the club very tightly with his left hand and very softly with his right, and he reached so far outward at address that his left arm and shaft appeared to be a straight line. He soled the clubhead almost two feet behind the ball and his swing motion was short and fast. While this completely self-taught motion appeared highly unusual, the results were amazing. He seemed to make pure square and centered contact every time he swung. **Sam Snead, Lee Trevino, Vijay Singh and countless golf historians considered Moe Norman to have been the greatest ball-striker in the history of golf. Tiger Woods said only two golfers in history "owned their swing": Ben Hogan and Moe Norman.**

I could very easily write an entire book about players who have competed and won on the highest level through employing completely self-taught unorthodox techniques. Bubba Watson, who won the 2012 Masters, would be such a player.

I could write another book about players you have never heard of. Players with enormous physical talent who spent their entire career working with swing coaches and computer-enhanced video cameras in an effort to develop an ideal golf swing. *Players who made the unfortunate mistake of believing golf was all about technique.* **The ball doesn't know how you swing and doesn't care. The ball only responds to the clubface at impact.**

How you swing is irrelevant. How you make contact with the ball is everything.

You swing faster than you can think, **so there is no reason to think while you're swinging.**

The human organism performs best in athletics when the conscious mind is turned off.
Dr. Bob Rotella

You're involved in the action and vaguely aware of it. I'd liken it to a sense of reverie – it is not merely mechanical, it is not only spiritual; it is something of both, on a different plane and a more remote one.
Arnold Palmer

While it's true that we consist of both body and mind, golfers tend to separate the two and associate themselves primarily with their conscious mind. When it comes to swinging a golf club, they view their physical body as a separate aspect of themselves that can never be completely trusted. ***Golfers think of their body as something that has to be continually told what to do.***

Bobby Jones wrote, *"I believe most sincerely that the impulse to steer, born of anxiety, is accountable for almost every really bad shot."*

Take a moment to think about that.

...the impulse to steer
...born of anxiety
...is accountable for almost every really bad shot

In other words:

...feeling the need to consciously manipulate the golf club
...due to the mistrust of your instinctual ability
...is the cause of almost every severe miss-hit

Conscious thought originates from 5 to 10% of the brain that's located in the frontal cortex area. This is the area of the brain where higher levels of thinking and goal formation take place. *What you need to understand is that this area of the brain is incapable of moving a muscle.* It's also limited in its ability to communicate to the part of the brain that does move muscles.

When you try to consciously manipulate your swing motion, **you're trying to move muscles from a part of the brain that can't efficiently do it.**

Motor activity is controlled *primarily* by an immensely efficient area of the brain known as the cerebellum - *the control center of your nervous system.* The cerebellum receives sensory, emotional, memory and language data from other areas of the brain through over 40 million nerve fibers. It then sends the electrical signals that run through your motor nerves and direct each of the myriad of muscle contractions needed to move your body, arms and hands and fingers in a very specific manner.

You have 639 skeletal muscles in your body and many of them are contracting in a specifically learned sequence during the 1.5 seconds of the swing motion. ***This is why it is correct to say that you swing faster than you can think.***

When you try to consciously manipulate your swing motion, you'll only succeed in disrupting the natural process and moving yourself off-balance. The greatest athletes think less while they are performing. They move with inner stillness. ***Free from the interference of conscious thought, their movements are balanced, effortless and spontaneous.***

When the great Yankee catcher Yogi Berra said, *"You cannot hit and think at the same time"*, he meant that, while at bat, you should do nothing more than take your stance, hold an intention, and *LET* your body respond to the ball.

The great Canadian golfer, George Kundsen, explains, *"...golf is a 'passive game,' one in which we LET most things happen rather than MAKE them happen."*

Tiger Woods writes, *"...it is almost as if I get out of the way and just LET it happen. I LET it happen. I do not MAKE it happen."*

When you think about performing a physical task while you're doing it, your mind is actually *separate* from the physical motion. While that statement appears to make no sense, it is true.

Thought **separates** your mind and body.

For example, when I typed the words on this page, my fingers moved without thought. My *intent* was to put my thoughts on paper and I was *aware* that I was typing, but I gave no thought to directing my fingers. I chose to allow my fingers to spontaneously type the words as the words came into my mind. The whole process was seamless. My body and mind operated in unison – *as one.*

If I tried to consciously guide my fingers I would have created *separation.* My mind would be instructing my fingers how to move, through conceptually assuming a position *separate* from my body. The effortless flow would have been destroyed and the process of typing would have been slow and error-filled.

This is how most golfers **try** to swing a golf club; their mind or ego **tries to guide the movements of their body.**

I found that idea was perfectly expressed in Steven Pressfield's wonderful book, *The Legend of Bagger Vance.* The mysterious caddie Bagger Vance tells his nervous golfing friend Rannulph Junah, *"You're in your head, Junah, I need you to come down into your hands. Listen to me. Intelligence, I have told you, does not reside in the brain but in the hands. LET them do the thinking, they're far wiser than you are."*

So does this mean you shouldn't think while playing golf? Not at all. In fact, your ability as a golfer is determined primarily by how well you *think* your way around the golf course.

The goal is to think **efficiently**.

You think most efficiently when you think exclusively about what you can consciously control – *shot selection, club selection, intention, and set up position;* while allowing what you cannot consciously control – *your swing motion* – to unfold naturally. **Your swing motion should not be guided by a stream of thoughts, but rather by the mere intention to make contact with the ball in a particular manner.**

It's your mind that needs guidance, **not your body.**

You don't TRY to swing in rhythm and balance, **you swing in rhythm and balance when you STOP TRYING.**

We must come to understanding that the very act of TRYING brings tension and rigidity.
Michael Hebron

The brain, while it does not swing the club, can stop the swing.
Dave Pelz

It's easy to swing in balance, and at your natural tempo, when you stay relaxed and swing without thought.

The practice of doing something without conscious effort (without thought) is referred to in Taoism as *wu wei*. In Eastern philosophy, it is considered to be the most efficient way to do anything. Action that is done with a mind free of thought and self consciousness is considered *supreme action*.

In the west, however, we tend to view the practice of doing something without conscious effort **to be lazy and ineffectual.**

We've been inbred with the Puritan work ethic: "success stems from hard work".

That perspective is quite apparent in the way we approach golf. We work hard at it. We over analyze, manipulate and force.

Ben Crenshaw wrote, *"Once I've started the putter in motion, it's as if it's swinging itself."* That is how you should perceive your full swing motion. With no controlling thoughts, you merely hold the intention to strike the ball in a particular manner, initiate the motion and allow your swing to unfold as spontaneously and naturally as possible.

When you move in balance and at your natural tempo, you don't feel anything; which is why you'll often hear players say they don't feel anything when they're swing their best. Their swing seems to move on its own, as if they weren't even trying.

After creating the intention to go for a walk, you *allow* your body to do it. It doesn't require a great deal of effort and you don't have to *tell* your body how to do it. And when you're walking, you do so in balance and at your natural tempo *because you're not thinking.* You don't *try* to walk in balance, you don't *think* about the pace of your stride, and you don't *feel* anything. It is as if your body is moving on its own, and it is.

Legendary swing instructor Ernest Jones wrote, *"Only when we insist on considering that balance comes about by a transfer of weight, by a conscious effort – or worse yet, series of efforts – does it become a perplexing and annoying problem."*

If you ever attend a PGA Tour event, be sure to visit the practice tee. You'll notice a wide variety of swing motions, each unfolding in a graceful and seemingly effortless manner. What each of these swings has in common is *balance*. You'll actually be able to sense the *balance* in their setup position, their swing motion, and their finish position.

At the local public driving range you'll observe just the opposite – a wide variety of lunging off-balanced swings, all being made with a great deal of effort.

Philosopher Alan Watts was a renowned interpreter of Zen Buddhism for the West. He once said, *"Really, the best meaning of wu-wei is 'don't force it'…This is like sailing a boat. It is more intelligent to sail a boat than to row it, even though sailing is a lazier way of doing it."* The best way to swing a golf club is without thought or effort; to sail instead of row!

When you swing without thought, you swing in balance and at your natural tempo; **and the game suddenly becomes much easier.**

Over analyzing swing mechanics **inhibits the natural learning process.**

A physicist can describe the perfect golf swing and write it down in scientific language, but the smart golfer doesn't read it. The smart golfer gives it to his opponents to contemplate.

Dr. Fran Pirozollo

Anyone who hopes to reduce putting – or any other department of the game of golf for that manner – to an exact science, is in for a serious disappointment, and will only suffer from the attempt.

Bobby Jones

With regards to playing better golf, a detailed analysis of swing mechanics serves no purpose. In fact, it most often leads to over-thinking, tension and conscious manipulation of the golf club.

These are the exact things **every golfer should strive to avoid.**

When you search outside yourself for swing guidance (books, magazines, videos), you're essentially searching for information you can use to *tell yourself* what to do. Any attempt to improve your ball-striking through **telling your body how to move** is the wrong approach.

As Michael Hebron writes in his book, *The Art and Zen of Learning Golf,* *"Telling the body how to do something with words is not the most effective way to improve performance. Our muscles don't understand English, and the thinking mind does not understand eye-hand coordination."*

Furthermore, the object in golf is not to move your body in a particular manner. The object is to create the impact conditions needed to send the ball to a specific target. Therefore, you don't need to focus on your swing motion; you need to focus on what you're attempting to do with the clubface.

In other words, instead of hoping to create desirable impact conditions through swinging in the manner someone else recommends, **determine the exact impact conditions you intend to create and let your body learn how to create them.**

Ball-striking is a motor skill, **not a swing motion.**

Your body learns to become more proficient at ball-striking the same way it learned to become more proficient at every other motor skill, **through repeated attempts and quality feedback.**

On each attempt, your job is to *re-identify* the specific objective (i.e. square and centered contact), carefully set-up to the ball in a manner that makes that objective easily achievable, and provide *quality* feedback (the impact conditions actually created). Other than that, you merely stay *present and aware* of what is happening.

You interfere with the learning process through incessant thinking; through continuously evaluating your results and changing your objective. When you attempt to *do it the right way* (force your body to adhere to the specific method you've deemed to be correct) and evaluate each effort as being *good or bad,* you encourage *in-swing thoughts* and slow the process of learning; almost to a stop.

Alan Watts writes, *"We should learn from our experiences (not someone else's). Our problem is that our power of thought enables us to construct symbols of things apart from the experience of things.*

The more you analyze swing mechanics the more controlling you become; **and the more controlling you become, the more you inhibit the natural process of learning.**

You manage your swing motion **through managing your set up position.**

*It is in this very way that a player should approach every shot on the course or even the practice tee. Let him always decide first upon the result he wants to produce; second, upon the precise manner in which to strike the ball; **and then let him place himself before the ball in such position that he knows he will be able to deliver the blow in this manner.***

Bobby Jones

All golfers should strive to develop the skill needed to produce *playable impact conditions* on a day-to-day basis. That skill is certainly obtainable, but it requires more than mere practice. It requires an understanding of the relationship between setup position, impact conditions and ball flight.

If you still don't fully understand how impact conditions create ball flight, you need to study the "About ball flight" section of this book until you do.

You also have to understand that your swing motion is going to change slightly on a daily basis. Yours, mine, Phil Mickelson's, everybody's golf swing is going to change slightly on a daily basis. Just accept it and learn to effectively deal with it.

As I wrote earlier in the book, *your swing motion is guided by and moves around your set up position.* **Therefore, you have the ability to "realign" your swing motion - on any given day - through slightly altering your set up position.**

With regards to altering your set up position, there are four primary areas of focus – **ball position, grip alignment, shoulder alignment, and stance.**

Because these areas interconnect and we all swing differently, it is impossible to make an absolute statement about how altering any one of them will influence YOUR specific impact conditions.

There are, however, **general rules of thumb** that you can use in the process of learning how the key aspects of YOUR set up position influence YOUR impact conditions.

*From the perspective of a **RIGHT HANDED PLAYER**, those would be as follows:*

GRIP ALIGNMENT

The alignment of your hands on the grip will influence the alignment of the clubface at impact.

- A **neutral grip** *(the **V-shape** formed between the thumb and forefinger of each hand pointing somewhere between the nose and right shoulder)* produces the best impact conditions for most golfers.

- A **strong grip** *(the **V-shape** formed between the thumb and forefinger of each hand points toward - or to the right of - the right shoulder)* will often produce a **clubface closed to the path of the clubhead** at impact.

- The **stronger** the grip at address the more **closed** the clubface will tend to be at impact. Golfers struggling with a push, fade, or slice will sometimes benefit through employing a **stronger grip**.

- A **weak grip** *(the **V-shape** formed between the thumb and forefinger of each hand points toward - or to the left of - the nose)* will often produce a **clubface open to the path of the clubhead** at impact.

- The **weaker** the grip at address the more **open** the clubface will tend to be at impact. Golfers struggling with a pull, draw, or hook will sometimes benefit through employing a **weaker grip.**

How YOU should align your hands on the grip can only be determined through a process of trial and error. There is no best way; there is only the way that best compliments YOUR swing motion.

SHOULDER ALIGNMENT

Where your shoulder-line points at address will directly influence where your shoulder-line will be pointing at impact; and there is an old saying in golf – *where the shoulders go, so goes the swing.*

- If at impact your shoulder-line points **significantly to the left** of your target line, you'll tend to swing the clubhead across the target line on an **outside-to-inside path**, *and your divots will point significantly to the left of your target.*

- Golfers attempting to hit a fade or slice will often set up with their shoulders aimed significantly to the **left of their target line** (to produce an *outside-to-inside clubhead path*) and **weaken their grip** (to produce an *open clubface* at impact).

- If at impact your shoulder-line points **significantly to the right** *of your target line*, you'll tend to swing the clubhead across the target line on an **inside-to-outside path,** *and your divots will point to the right of your target.*

- Golfers attempting to hit a draw or hook will often set up with their shoulders aimed significantly to the **right of their target line** (to produce an *inside-to-outside clubhead path*) and **strengthen their grip** (to produce a *closed clubface at impact*).

- If at impact your shoulder-line is **roughly parallel** to the target line you'll tend to swing the clubhead toward the target – **and your divots will point in the general direction of the target.**

- Golfers struggling to swing their clubhead toward their target (divots pointing significantly to the left or right) will very often benefit through **altering the alignment of their shoulders** at address.

Because the alignment of your shoulders significantly influences the path of the clubhead, you should always be aware of the direction your shoulders are pointed at address.

Don't confuse the alignment of your shoulders with **shoulder tilt.** At address, your right shoulder will be slightly lower than your left shoulder because your right hand is lower on the shaft. At impact, the slide of the lower body toward the target will pull the right shoulder even lower.

BALL POSITION

Where you position the ball in your stance affects the quality of impact in many ways; including the alignment of the clubface, the path of the clubhead, the angle of approach, and the face impact location.

To understand the importance of ball position, you need to think about how the clubhead travels through the hitting area. It moves along a **tilted vertical arc** that resembles a tilted hula-hoop; and as the clubhead is swinging along that arc and toward the target, the toe of the clubface is continuously rotating forward.

Take a few slow motion practice swings and observe the **tilted hula-hoop** *path of the clubhead* and the **counterclockwise** *rotation of the clubface* independently. Pretending that you were attempting to hit a straight shot, notice that the clubhead will be traveling down the target line for only an instant; just as the clubface will be square to the target line for only an instant. **Ideally**, both of these will occur at exactly the same time – **at the moment of impact.** That, however, will seldom happen.

You can't time ideal impact conditions because the swing unfolds far too quickly. You can, however, increase the likelihood of making square contact **through adjusting your ball position and grip.**

Through keeping your head relatively steady and not over-swinging, and making a balanced swing, you can teach yourself to strike the ground (start your divot) in just about the same place every time. For most golfers, that place will *naturally* occur just forward of mid-stance.

Ideally, the clubface will strike the ball an *instant* before it strikes the ground. Therefore, your ball should be positioned where your divots normally start. For wedges and short irons, that might be close to middle of your stance; as the shafts become progressively longer you might notice your divots moving *slightly forward* (toward the target).

Once you determine the ideal ball position (relative to your swing arc), you can adjust the **alignment of the clubface** through adjusting the **alignment of your grip**. If your clubface tends to be always **open to the path of the clubhead** (you're always fading or slicing), you might be able to square it through slightly **strengthening** your grip. If your clubface tends to be always **closed to the path of the clubhead** (you're always hooking), you might be able to square it through slightly **weakening** your grip.

- **If the ball is positioned too far back in the stance,** it will tend to be struck with a more descending blow, the clubface will tend to be **open to the target line**, and the

113

clubhead will tend to be traveling on a *line aimed to the right of the target*. *As a result, this ball position will often produce a push, a push fade, or even a push slice*.

- Golfers struggling with a push, fade or slice (***open clubface at impact***), will sometimes benefit through moving the ball slightly forward in their stance (toward the target). This adjustment gives the clubface more time to rotate toward a ***square position***.

- Some golfers prefer to hit draws or hooks through positioning the ball back in their stance (to facilitate an ***inside-to-outside path***) and significantly strengthen their grip (to ***close the clubface***).

- **If the ball is positioned too far forward in the stance,** it will tend to be struck with a less descending blow, the clubface will tend to be ***closed to the target line***, and the clubhead will tend to be traveling on a ***line aimed to the left of the target***. *As a result, this ball position will often produce a pull, a pull draw, or even a pull hook*.

- Golfers struggling with a pull, draw, or hook (***closed clubface at impact***) will sometimes benefit through moving the ball slightly back in their stance (away from the target). As a result, impact may occur *before* the clubface rotates to a significantly ***closed position***.

- Some golfers prefer to hit a fade or slice through positioning the ball *forward in their stance* (to facilitate an ***outside-to-inside path***) and significantly *weakening their grip* (to keep the ***clubface open***).

STANCE

How you position your feet relative to the target line will influence the length of your backswing, your swing plane, and the clubhead's angle of approach.

- A *square stance* (both feet positioned an equal distance from the target line) is considered to be a neutral position. *Some players believe they achieve more consistent impact conditions through playing all of their shots from a square stance.*

- A *closed stance* (rear foot is drawn back and positioned further from target line than the forward foot) encourages a longer backswing, a flatter swing plane and more sweeping strike.

- The longer clubs (driver and fairway metals) are designed to be played with a more sweeping strike. *For that reason, some players prefer to play their longer clubs from a closed stance.*

- *Many* golfers who struggle with their flexibility, will employ a *closed stance* to create a fuller backswing.

- An *open stance* (forward foot is drawn back and positioned further from the target line than rear foot) encourages a restricted backswing, a more upright swing plane and a more descending strike.

- The shorter clubs (wedges on short irons) are designed to be played with a more descending strike. *For that reason, some players prefer to play their wedges and short irons from an open stance.*

- When hitting the ball from the rough, better players try to minimize the debris (grass and dirt) caught between the ball and the clubface through striking the ball with a more descending blow. This becomes easier through positioning the ball back (toward their rear foot) and *opening their stance.*

Effectively managing your set up position on both a **shot-to-shot** and **day-to-day** basis **is an art few golfers master**

Hitting a golf ball effectively is not easy, **but it's not nearly as difficult as most golfers make it.**

The swing is the easiest part of golf. Once you've got the right grip and if you hold your head steady, it is almost impossible to swing badly.
Arnold Palmer

So many people try to make golf harder than it really is.
Annika Sorenstam

Modern golf clubs are very light, require very little effort to swing, and are designed to make hitting a golf ball as easy as possible. Furthermore, the golf ball doesn't move, it just sits there and waits for you to hit it. So why do most golfers struggle with their ball-striking?

It's because they MAKE ball-striking more difficult than it really is. There are many ways to do that, here are the most popular:

- **Pay no attention to how you grip the club.**

  A poor grip will almost guarantee that the clubface will not be square at impact.

- **Pay no attention to where you position the ball in your stance or how you align yourself.**

116

This will insure that you'll almost never swing the clubhead straight down the target line.

- **Always try to hit the ball as far as possible**

This will insure added tension and a wildly inconsistent lunging off-balance motion.

- **Try to consciously manipulate your swing motion.**

This will insure that your swing motion remains forever off-tempo, out of rhythm and off-balance.

Those four practices alone make hitting a golf ball effectively almost impossible, **but most golfers don't stop there:**

- **Address the ball with a great deal of tension in your hands and body.**

This will effectively stifle any hand-eye coordination that you've developed. It will also greatly restrict your range of motion and inhibit your ability to rotate the clubface to a square position at impact.

- **While you're swinging, think about something else.**

While swinging, think about your score, what other players are doing, where the ball might go after you hit it, or anything else completely unrelated to the goal of making square and centered contact; this will insure that you almost never make square and centered contact.

- **Never aim at a specific target.**

Learning how to hit the ball to a specific target becomes impossible when you never aim at a specific target.

- **Continuously change your swing.**

Immediately implementing every swing tip you read or hear about should guarantee a complete lack of progress.

Hitting a golf ball effectively becomes much easier, **once the golfer stops making it almost impossible.**

PART SIX
UNDERSTANDING HOW TO
PLAY BETTER GOLF

It is nothing new or original to say that golf should be played one stroke at a time. But it took me years to realize it.

Bobby Jones

Focus on what you can consciously control, **and forget about everything else.**

...there must be no mental daisy-picking
while the shot is being played.

Bobby Jones

Developing your ability as a shotmaker requires that, during the few seconds of the shotmaking process, you focus *exclusively* on what you can consciously control.

There are five consciously controllable aspects of shotmaking; I refer to each of them as a *playing skill*.

SHOT SELECTION

You can carefully evaluate the circumstances, consider your options, and determine the highest percentage shot.

CLUB SELECTION

You can consider your choices and select the club that allows for an appropriate margin of error.

INTENTION

You can center your focus and form a single-minded intention to create the exact shot you selected.

SETUP POSITION

You can take the time to consciously setup to the ball in the manner that will allow you to most easily create that exact shot.

SWING FOCUS

While maintaining your intention to strike the ball in a particular manner, you can choose to allow your swing to unfold without thought or effort.

Most golfers struggle with their shotmaking because they **allow** their thoughts to drift into areas that are both beyond their control and irrelevant to the shot at hand.

While trying to play a shot, they might also think about:

How other golfers are playing

What other golfers are thinking

Trying to impress another golfer

Trying to not embarrass them self in front of another golfer

What might happen to the ball after it leaves the clubface

What their swing is going to look like

What their final score on the hole (or for the round) might be

The results of the their last shot

A bad break

What happened the last time they faced a similar shot

An excuse for why they're not playing well

And these are just the thoughts related to golf.

Their shot-making is inconsistent because they're unable to stay fully engaged with the shot at hand. Instead, they **allow** their mind to wander.

Forgetting about what you can't consciously control **is the first step to becoming better at what you can consciously control.**

You become a better golfer through **developing your APPROACH to shotmaking.**

---

*Do not let what you can't do
Interfere with what you can do.*

John Wooden

The *five playing skills* are again – *shot selection, club selection, intention, set up position, and swing focus.* Collectively I refer to them as your *approach to shotmaking.*

It is your approach to shotmaking **that defines your ability as a golfer.**

Developing any one of the playing skills will have an immediate positive effect on your game. But the *synergetic effect* realized through developing all five skills is really quite amazing. Not only will your scores drop significantly, they'll do so with seemingly no effort.

Effortless improvement is realized when you shift your focus from your score to the *process* of producing a specific golf shot; *when you become fully engaged in the moment, with no concern about what happened in the past or what might happen in the future.*

A golfer who has an effective *approach to shotmaking* is usually considered to be an anomaly; a player who routinely scores lower than his natural ability, his equipment, or the appearance of his swing might suggest. In truth he is simply a golfer who has acquired a better than average understanding of *how the game is best played.*

The average golfer, on the other hand, is forever hampered by his *limited understanding* of the game and *ineffective approach to shotmaking.* As a result, he rarely scores to the level of his talent.

123

I've discussed each of the playing skills throughout this book. Let's take a quick review:

SHOT SELECTION

On every shot, there are two objectives. The first is to advance the ball into the hole or as close to the hole as possible. The second is to minimize the possibility of hitting into a penalizing or difficult situation. With those two objectives in mind, the skilled golfer determines the *highest percentage shot.*

Four key ideas associated with optimizing your *shot selection:*

• Hitting into a penalizing or difficult situation will most typically hurt your score far more than a good shot will help your score. For that reason, avoiding these situations has to be your *top priority.*

• Regardless of your level of play, you don't hit the ball as straight as you think you do. For that reason, aiming to the center or safe side of fairways and greens will usually be your best option.

• **Y**our ball-striking ability will change slightly from day to day. On days when your ball-striking is below average, your approach to shot selection will have to be even more conservative than normal.

• If the shot you've selected requires perfect execution, you've probably selected the wrong shot. Your average shot is going to be a slight mishit, everyone's is, so accept it and prepare for it.

• Attempting a spectacular recovery shot from a difficult situation (trees, deep rough, deep fairway bunkers, etc.) will almost always add needless shots to your score. Getting the ball back into play *in one shot* should be the **top priority.** The reward gained from *perfectly executing the shot* will seldom be worth the risk.

With aggressive shot selection, you're forced to **continually** hit better than average golf shots to avoid hitting into the penalizing or difficult situations that you **continually** bring into play.

When you optimize your shot selection you only have to hit average shots to play great golf.

CLUB SELECTION

The average golfer selects a club based solely on their distance from the pin. The problem is that they believe they hit the ball farther than they actually do. As a result, they chronically **under-club** themselves and seldom get the ball to the green, much less to the hole. This is the reason hazards positioned in front of greens catch a lot of balls, while hazards positioned behind greens are seldom visited.

Once again, your average shot is going to be a slight mishit. As a result, the clubface is going to turn slightly at impact and the ball is not going to carry quite as far as you might have intended. That is not a problem as long as you prepare for it through **never under-clubbing.**

Seven key ideas associated with optimizing your **club selection:**

• Strive to do more than just get the ball to the green, strive to get the ball all the way to the hole. Then select the club that will allow you to do that with the **least amount of effort.**

• Always base your club selection on **average carry distance.** That is the average distance the ball will carry with a particular club when you swing at your normal effort (80 to 85%).

• To achieve your maximum potential carry distance with a particular golf club you'll need to make perfect square and centered contact. Because that will rarely happen, **you should seldom choose a club based on its maximum potential carry distance.**

- When you **under-club** yourself you're forced to **over-swing**, which increases the likelihood of a more severe mishit.

- When closer to the hole, golfers typically choose a club with too much loft. **Around the green**, *whenever possible*, select a club that will produce **less carry and more roll**. This will increase your chance of actually getting the ball **to the hole.**

- An uphill lie will increase your *effective loft* and a downhill lie will decrease your *effective loft*. Therefore, even around the greens, consider playing a less lofted club from an uphill lie and a higher lofted club from a downhill lie.

- If you lose confidence with a particular club on a particular day, select a different club. A lack of confidence breeds anxiety, tension and conscious manipulation.

Optimizing your club selection will require that you chart the **average carry distance** (with your normal 80 to 85% effort) of every club in your bag – *lob wedge through driver.*

INTENTION

Your *intention* is the intangible aspect of shot-making. Because it can't be seen or felt, **it is seldom even considered.** That's a huge mistake because nothing will influence your swing motion more than your intention.

Seven key ideas associated with optimizing your **intention:**

- Your intention will greatly influence your swing motion, so you have to be **consciously aware** of *exactly* what your intention is.

- Your intention should always be related to your target or the impact conditions you're attempting to create (external); never related to the movements of your body (internal).

- Your intention should always be positive. Focus only on what you *do want to happen* and give no consideration at all to what you *don't want to happen.*

- Make your intention as specific as possible. Don't aim at a general area, give your body a *very specific target.*

- Be comfortable with the intention you've created. Your body cannot effectively respond to your intention if you lack confidence. If you *feel* you don't posses the ability to achieve your objective (on that day or in that moment), choose a different objective. *Listen to your body and allow it to influence your decisions.*

- Always employ some technique to *strengthen* your intention. You might visualize the flight of the shot, visualize the ball in your target area, sense the shot through practice swings, or merely verbalize your intention. Experiment and discover the strengthening technique that works best for you.

- Maintain your single intention *throughout the shot-making process.* Allow it to guide how you set up to the ball and how you swing the club.

Jack Nicklaus felt the 50% of the success of a golf shot was related to his ability to form a strong intention.

SET UP POSITION

Your golf swing is guided by and moves around your set up position. To consistently achieve desirable impact conditions, you have to learn to consistently grip the club and set up to the ball in the manner that best compliments the *specific impact conditions you're attempting to create.*

To some degree, everyone swings differently; so to some degree, everyone should grip the club and setup to the ball differently – regardless of the attempted shot. The goal is to setup to the ball in the manner that would allow YOU to most easily create YOUR desired impact conditions.

127

Three key ideas associated with optimizing your **setup position**:

- To set the stage for a natural swing motion you have to **quiet your mind** and **relax your body.** Your setup routine has to include those two objectives.

- Allow your intention to create **specific impact conditions** be the sole guide as to how you setup to the ball. Visualize the impact conditions you're attempting to create, understand how you're going to create them, and allow your body to settle into a comfortable and complementary position.

- You'll sense if you're not properly set-up. If you feel uncomfortable back away and start again.

To do this, you have to acquire the understanding of how impact conditions create ball flight and how the key aspects of YOUR setup position (ball position, grip alignment, shoulder alignment, and stance) influence YOUR ability to strike the ball in a particular manner.

SWING FOCUS

It takes less than two seconds to swing a golf club. How you're focused during that time is critically important. For that reason, you have to manage and continuously monitor your thoughts.

Five key ideas associated with optimizing your **swing focus**:

- **Always swing without thought.** Your swing unfolds best when guided merely by your intention to strike the ball in a specific manner.

- Always swing with trust and confidence. Accept that your body is far wiser than you are, and **mentally step aside.**

- **Maintain high expectations**. Doubts only serve to inhibit motor skills; shake doubts off before addressing the ball.

- Swing fully and sense your body moving. Be aware of your entire motion but make no effort to *judge* or *consciously control* the movements.

- Maintain relaxed and *uniform grip pressure* throughout the swing motion. Eliminate effort and allow your body to move freely.

Developing your approach to shotmaking is a *slow, continuous, changing process* that requires commitment and the willingness to become fully present and aware of what's happening in the moment. It requires that you understand and accept *what can be consciously controlled* and *what cannot be consciously controlled*; and therefore, when to be fully engaged and when to fully let go. A highly effective approach to shotmaking is an art that requires constant maintenance.

To the serious golfer, the rewards of developing and maintaining an effective approach to shotmaking **will far exceed the effort.**

Begin every round with the same goal, **to play EVERY SHOT with a high degree of purpose.**

The real way to enjoy playing golf is to take pleasure not in the score, but in the execution of strokes.
Bobby Jones

You'll hit fewer poor golf shots (and lower your average score) when, on every shot, you give appropriate consideration to what you can effectively control - *shot selection, club selection, intention, setup position, and swing focus.*

Because that's a lot to consider in a short period of time, you need to develop a *shotmaking routine* that makes the process almost automatic. Whether it's a driver, full iron shot, pitch, chip or putt, your personal routine never changes.

For most skilled players, the routine is something similar to this:

First, they take the necessary time to carefully evaluate their circumstances, determine the highest percentage shot, and select the most appropriate club.

Second, they establish the single positive intention to create that specific shot and employ some technique to strengthen that intention *before addressing the ball.*

Third, understanding the impact conditions they'll need to create, they relax their body, quiet their mind, and proceed to set up to the ball in a manner that will allow them to most easily create those conditions.

Finally, they mentally step aside and allow their swing to be guided only by their intention to strike the ball in a specific manner. Instead of thinking, they choose to swing with confidence and trust.

Before every round, you should commit to the same goal - *to play every shot with a high degree of purpose.* You can accomplish that goal through employing the same all-inclusive approach to every shot. As Tiger woods states, *"All I do is stay in my same routine...do everything the same."*

The key to a successful routine is to **COMPLETE** each step **BEFORE** moving on the next step.

Most golfers have no shotmaking routine and no game plan. As a result, each shot is approached in a different manner and given a different degree of attention. Quite often, they get fully set up to the ball before determining exactly what they intend to do.

Finalizing your intention *after* assuming your address position obviously makes no sense at all. Yet, this is how most golfers play. It's certainly how most golfers putt.

Make it your goal to never set up to the ball BEFORE first **strengthening your intention to create a specific shot, quieting your mind and relaxing your body.**

Barring unusual circumstances, the entire shot-making routine should take 15 to 30 seconds. Most of it can be accomplished while waiting for your playing partners to hit their shots.

In golf, every shot counts the same. Therefore, every shot deserves the same consideration. Giving a single shot 15 to 30 seconds of organized thought is not difficult. Playing every shot in the round *with that degree of purpose* requires a discipline that few golfers develop. They think of it as requiring too much effort. But how much effort does it really take to *think* for a few seconds? You're always going to determine the shot you're going to play, select a club, create some sort of intention, setup to the ball in some manner, and think about something while you're swinging.

The question is, do you want to approach the endeavors mindlessly or with purpose? Do you want to hit more poor shots or fewer poor shots?

Your ball-striking will improve as you **learn to mentally step aside.**

Thinking instead of acting is the number-one golf disease.
SAM SNEAD

Success depends almost entirely on how effectively you learn to manage the game's two ultimate adversaries, the course and yourself.
JACK NICKLAUS

When in college, I drove a small car with a manual transmission. Lost in the music continually blaring from my radio, I drove on congested freeways and through busy city traffic. I stayed alert and fully aware of the changing traffic conditions, but I operated the car ***subconsciously***. As I steered through traffic, I worked the clutch with my left foot, worked the break and gas pedals with my right foot, and shifted gears with my right hand; but I didn't *consciously try to guide any of these movements*. I just stayed alert, ***observed*** what was happening around me and let my body ***seamlessly responded*** to those observations.

I certainly didn't want to stall my car, shift into the wrong gear, miss a turn, or get into an accident; but I didn't give those possibilities any consideration at all.

So if I can mentally step aside and fearlessly allow my body/subconscious mind to drive my car 70 miles per hour through heavy freeway traffic, why do I find it so difficult to step aside and fearlessly allow the same body/subconscious mind hit a golf shot?

Virtually every great ball-striker claims to swing without thought, and virtually every poor golfer can't stop thinking. While professional golfers and sports psychologists address this issue routinely, I believe the great Moe Norman spoke about it with the most passion.

Moe Norman is widely recognized as possibly the greatest ball-striker in the history of the game. In listening to his interviews on *Youtube.com*, I'd hear him repeatedly say, *"What is the longest walk in golf? It's from the practice tee to the first tee. I don't care if it's only 10 yards, it's the longest walk in golf. Winners take their swing with them. Losers don't"*. Moe believed that on the golf course most players became severely hampered by fear and self-doubt.

Moe defined a good golfer as one who, *"...can hit the ball to a defined target area with the least amount of effort, but an alert mind of indifference."* He also said that, *"The only way you're going to play golf to your full potential is by playing subconscious golf."*

In other words, Moe felt that I should swing my golf club the same way I drove my car while in college – subconsciously, with little effort and no consideration of the negative possibilities.

Throughout this book, I've tried to stress the importance of becoming better at what you can *consciously control* while allowing what you can't effectively control (your swing motion) to unfold **completely free of thought**.

It is not easy, however, to turn a **racing mind** on and off. That is why it is so essential for the golfer to approach the process of shotmaking from a state of **calm indifference.**

Lee Trevino was famous for talking incessantly on the golf course, but he said he did so for a specific reason – **to stay calm.** Talking was Lee's way of staying comfortable and relaxed **between shots.** Through maintaining relaxed and comfortable throughout the round, it was easier for Lee to center his focus during the actual shotmaking process and quiet his mind when swinging. I assure you, there was no idle chatter going on while the shot was being played. Every aspect of Lee Trevino's **approach to shotmaking** was obviously highly efficient.

100 years ago, Harry Vardon was considered to be the best golfer in the world. He won 62 tournaments (including six British Opens) and he once won 14 tournaments in a row. Harry wrote, *"To play well you must feel tranquil and at peace"*.

All golfers should strive to **swing their club** with what Moe Norman defined as **an alert mind of indifference.**

Remember that **preparing to swing** is a **conscious process**, but the swing itself is not. On the golf course, you **consciously prepare to swing** through selecting the highest percentage shot, choosing the club that allows for an appropriate margin of error, forming a strong intention to create that exact shot, and setting up to the ball in the manner that allows you to most easily create the desired impact conditions.

Then, knowing that you've done everything you can do, **you mentally step aside and LET your body effortlessly respond to your intention.**

Another of Moe's favorite sayings was, *"LET the body enjoy the shot. That's the biggest word in golf, LET"*. In other words, ***let go*** of all fear and doubt, clear your mind, and swing with confidence and high expectations.

In truth, there is absolutely no reason not to. **It is the only way you'll ever play to your full potential.**

Practice with the specific intent of **becoming a better golfer.**

All my life I've tried to hit practice shots with great care. I try to have a clear-cut purpose in mind on every swing. I always practice as I intend to play. And I learned long ago that there is a limited number of shots you can hit effectively before losing your concentration on your basic objectives

Jack Nicklaus

Practice is necessary, but it is not sufficient. Smart practice is what golfers need to do to improve.

Dave Pelz

For practice to be effective, you have to be aware of what you're doing. Just aiming at the same target, maintaining your stance, and mindlessly repeating the same golf swing, does not improve your ability to *play* golf. **Golf is not about the continuous repetition of the same motion.**

You don't practice to become a robot,you practice to develop the **motor skills** and **confidence** to become a better shotmaker.

Golf is about shotmaking; about creating specific flight patterns and hitting the ball specific distances. Therefore, your practice time should be devoted to two goals, improving your **approach to shotmaking** (your five playing skills) and **expanding your arsenal of shots.**

And because approximately 60% of your shots on the golf course are going to be within 60 yards of the green, the majority of your practice time should be devoted to developing your short game.

IMPROVING YOUR APPROACH TO SHOTMAKING

You improve your approach to shotmaking through developing an **all-inclusive shotmaking routine** and applying that routine to **each practice shot.** After each shot, step away and *prepare* to hit the next shot as if you were *preparing* to hit a shot on the golf course; with the exact same intensity.

Effective shotmaking requires that you manage your thinking; that skill can be developed on the practice range.

EXPANDING YOUR ARSENAL OF SHOTS

Expanding your arsenal of shots is relatively easy, AFTER you acquire the understanding of how impact conditions create ball flight *(outlined in the "About ball flight" section of this book)*. With that understanding, you don't need an instructor to teach you how to hit a particular golf shot, you just keep repeating the same three steps.

First, you determine the exact shot you wish to create and identify the impact conditions that would produce that shot.

Second, you select the appropriate club and setup to the ball in a manner that makes those conditions easy to produce.

Third, you swing confidently, observe the results, and determine the impact conditions you actually created (through analyzing the ball flight, divot, and face impact location).

Through repeated attempts, quality feedback, and (if needed) slight adjustments to your setup position, you can develop the skill needed to create any shot. And when you learn how to create the same shot with a variety of clubs and methods, you're on your way to becoming a great shotmaker.

The more you practice, the more you'll gain the **confidence** needed to create these shots on the golf course.

Teaching yourself how to create the three basic trajectories (high, medium and low) and the three basic flight patterns (slicing, straight, and hooking), will be a very rewarding use of your practice time.

Don't be concerned with someone else's opinion of *the right way* to do anything. The *right approach* is ALWAYS the approach that works best for you; which will generally differ from the approach that works best for anyone else.

The only constants are related to impact conditions; **the laws of physics don't change.**

To hit the ball an exact distance with a particular ball flight, all of us have to deliver the clubface to the ball in the same manner; you, me, Tiger Woods, all of us. There are, however, infinite ways (swings/methods) that will deliver the clubface to the ball in that exact manner. The particular swing or method each of us chooses to employ is irrelevant.

PRODUCTIVE PRACTICE

The secret to productive practice is to stay fully present and aware of what you're doing. Furthermore, every shot should be struck with a specific purpose. It doesn't matter how many balls you hit or how many hours you practice.

For most golfers, a series of short highly focused practice sessions are far more productive than a single session of several hours. As Jack Nicklaus writes, *"...I learned long ago that there is a limited number of shots you can hit effectively before losing your concentration on your basic objectives."*

It's the **degree of awareness** that you give to **each shot** that determines the productivity of the practice session.

FINAL THOUGHTS

Ask yourself how many shots you would have saved if you never lost your temper, never got down on yourself, always developed a strategy before you hit, and always played within your capabilities.

Jack Nicklaus

Four ideas **that I hope you'll fully embrace.**

I've covered a lot of ideas in a relatively short book. The four foundation ideas that I hope you'll fully embrace are:

To lower your average score, you don't need to hit the ball farther, buy new equipment, or change your golf swing; all you have to do is improve your *playing skills*. When you stop developing your *playing skills*, you stop improving as a golfer.

Your five playing skills are: shot selection, club selection, intention, set up position, and swing focus. Together they constitute your *approach to shotmaking* and define your ability as a golfer.

Improving your playing skills does not require great talent or months of practice, *because each skill is within your complete conscious control*. All that is required is that you expand your understanding of golf and *effectively apply* what you learn.

When you improve your approach to shotmaking, develop an *effective shotmaking routine*, and apply that routine to every shot in the round, your average score will drop. Regardless of your level of play.

The most difficult part of improvement, **is simply staying on the path.**

There are no short cuts to any place worth going.
Beverly Sills

The difficulty lies not in the new ideas, but in escaping the old ones, which ramify, for those brought up as most of us have, into every corner of our minds.
John Maynard Keynes

Time and again, I've watched players improve their approach to shotmaking and significantly lower their average score, only to fully regress after once again becoming overly concerned with the appearance of their swing, the distance they hit the ball, or the quality of their equipment.

To describe this common occurrence, I use the metaphor of a driver who has been given a road map to his destination. As he travels down the freeway, getting ever closer to his goal, he can't resist the temptation of taking a short cut, to get there a little quicker. Unfortunately every short cut just leads him all the way back to his starting point.

When golfers start to become overly concerned with their swing, their equipment, or the distance they hit the ball, they're just looking for short cuts. And when they become preoccupied with these areas their focus shifts, all improvement stops, and their playing skills slowly diminish. Eventually their level of play will return to where it was when they started.

The moral of my story is simple - *stay on the path until you reach your goal.* That goal being to always play to your full potential (whatever that might be) on a given day. Don't be tempted by short cuts, because there are no short cuts.

First, you learn to better understand the game and slowly develop your approach to shotmaking. Then, you progressively mold your new approach into an effective shotmaking routine and apply that routine to every shot in your round. How fast you progress and how good of a golfer you ultimately become is dependent only on the amount of time and effort you're willing to donate to the goal of improving each of your five playing skills.

How fast you progress and how good of a golfer you ultimately become is dependent only on **the amount of time and effort you're willing to donate to the goal of improving each of your five playing skills.**

When working with golfers, I have only one rule; *I require that they apply their shotmaking routine to every shot in practice and every shot in every round.* That single rule insures the development of every aspect of their game.

Good luck and I look forward to hearing from you.

Phil Moore
PhilMooreGolf.com